the QUIZ ?life

Marina Khidekel

DELACORTE PRESS

Published by Delacorte Press
an imprint of Random House Children's Books
a division of Random House, Inc.
New York

DELACORTE PRESS and colophon are registered trademarks of
Random House, Inc.

Visit us on the Web! www.randomhouse.com/teens
Educators and librarians, for a variety of teaching tools,
visit us at www.randomhouse.com/teachers

Library of Congress Cataloging-in-Publication Data

Khidekel, Marina.
  The quiz life / by Marina Khidekel. — 1st ed.
     p. cm.
  ISBN 978-0-375-84263-4 (trade pbk.) — ISBN 978-0-375-94063-7 (glb)
1. Teenage girls—Psychology—Miscellanea—Juvenile literature.
2. Teenage girls—Social conditions—Miscellanea—Juvenile literature.
3. Interpersonal relations in adolescence—Miscellanea—Juvenile
literature. 4. Questions and answers. I. Title.
  HQ798.K485 2008
  155.5'33—dc22
                              2007002753

Book design by Vikki Sheatsley

Printed in the United States of America
10 9 8 7 6 5 4 3 2 1
First Edition

Introduction

What's your life like right now? Are you wondering if the guy you like likes you back? Trying to be a great friend? Obsessing over who you really are and what kind of person you're meant to become? Just hoping to have some fun?

If you answered yes to any of these questions, you're living what I call the Quiz Life, because you don't just let things be—you're the kind of girl who wonders why things are the way they are. I think every girl, whether she lives in a small town or a big city or somewhere in between, wants to look inside herself and figure out who she is. Myself included! Luckily, quizzes can help you learn all that—and have fun doing it!

Just so you know, I'm the kind of person who puts a lot of value on realness. I appreciate it when a friend is up-front with me rather than just telling me what she *thinks* I want to hear (even if I'm not thrilled with the truth). And when things are dumbed down, my eyes usually glaze over. So I try to always tell it like it is. The advice in the quizzes you're about to take is exactly what I'd give to my good friends or the younger sister I never had. And you know what? I'd love it if you guys reading this would be my honorary sisters. It's time to uncover tons of new stuff about *every* part of your life. So come on, get cracking! It's good to live the Quiz Life!

XX,
Marina

Contents

1) Is he trying to tell you he likes you? 1

2) How do you deal with drama? 6

3) How independent are you? 12

4) What's your band role? 18

5) Are you too picky?. 22

6) What makes people jealous of you?. 27

7) Are you a go-getter?. 33

8) What movie-theater snack are you? 39

9) What makes you hot to guys? 43

10) Are you a good friend? 48

11) What strength sets you apart? 53

12) Who's your comic-book hero? 60

13) Is he shady? 64

14) Are you too predictable? 69

15) Do you act your age? 74

16) What kind of girlfriend are you? 79

17) Are you a risk taker? 83

18) Are boys taking over your brain? 89

19) Is she a true friend? 94

20) Are you a downer? 99

21) What kind of starlet would you be? 105

22) Are you getting through to him? 109

23) How competitive are you? 115

24) How high maintenance are you? 120

25) What big city should you live in? 125

26) Are you toying with your guy? 129

27) What's your friendship role? 134

28) Are you in a rut? 139

29) How gullible are you? 145

30) Are you too plugged in? 150

31) What kind of flirt are you? 155

32) Do you live for gossip? 161

33) What kind of dreamer are you? 166

34) Is your friend holding you back? 171

35) How do you party? 176

36) What role does he play in your life? 180

37) Are you a material girl? 185

38) Do you freak guys out? 189

39) What do people say behind your back? 194

40) Should you break up with your friend? 199

41) How well do you know yourself? 205

Is he trying to tell you he likes you?

Sometimes trying to read guys is like trying to decipher ancient Egyptian hieroglyphics—crazy confusing. Take this quiz to decode the signals your crush is giving.

1 Do mutual friends tell you he mentions you when you're not around?

A Yeah, kind of a lot. Actually, he just asked if you'll be at a party your bff is throwing.

B Once in a while, but kind of in a roundabout way, like "What's the deal with her?"

C Not really.

2 **When you're talking to him, you notice that he usually:**

A Looks down or to the side, and gives you mostly one-word answers.

B Keeps looking at you, looking away, and then looking back—but rarely right into your eyes.

C Locks eyes with you and holds your gaze—and tilts his head like he's really hearing you out.

3 **You run into him while shopping with your mom. . . . Embarrassing! He'd be most likely to:**

A Stop and chat for a while, asking your mom tons of questions and totally winning her over.

B Wave and say, "Hey, how are you?"

C Quickly give a nod of recognition and keep walking.

4 **How often does he mention the other girls in his life to you?**

A Um, never. You've never heard him talk about anyone else he's dated or is interested in.

B Pretty rarely, and when he does, it's almost always about how some girl has a crush on him.

C Almost every time you guys talk, he brings up how he has a crush on so-and-so, or how hot some girl (who isn't you) is.

5 **If you bring up a guy you hooked up with a while ago, he'd:**

A Probably call him a jerk or say something else mean about him.

B Change the subject pretty fast.

C Say something like "That guy's cool," then talk about a girl *he* hooked up with.

Mostly As: Loud and clear.

This guy's sending some pretty direct signals that he sees you as more than just a friend or lab partner (Hello! He's anti every-other-guy-you've-dated!). The only question is why he's keeping silent about it. Chances are he's just shy or he's scared you'll reject him if he makes an outright play for you. Let him know you're open to moving beyond friend territory by getting him alone and saying something like "Have you ever thought about us being more than friends?" He'll feel comfortable enough to fess up, and then you'll both know what the other is trying to say.

Mostly Bs: Mixed signals.

Who can blame you for being confused? Mr. Vague here is acting like he couldn't be open with his feelings toward you if his life depended on it. What's probably going on is he's just insecure about whether you're into him, and trying to test the waters. If you do like him (and you're both single), then the only way to stop wondering how he feels is to make a move. Ask him if he wants to do something one-on-one, like grabbing some pizza. If he says yes, consider him interested—but flirt with caution to protect your heart. If he says no, he's not ready to be more than friends, and knowing that will free you to move on to someone who is.

He doesn't seem interested in moving into relationship territory, and if you're cool with that, then keep on being friends (or teammates or whatever). If the idea that he's not into you "like that" *stings,* then keep your distance for a while so you can let yourself move on without pining every time you see him (ouch!). Yeah, it's fun to have a crush, but if you know there's no chance of it turning into something real, it's not healthy to dwell on it. Instead, focus on hanging out with your other friends or doing something you're great at, like perfecting your school play performance. That way you'll get your mind off him *and* realize that your life rocks without someone to pine over—until your next crush comes along, anyway!

2

How do you deal with
DRAMA?

Life happens, and it doesn't always go smoothly. When things get rocky, does your reaction bring on an avalanche?

1] **Two of your friends are in a marathon cold-shoulder war, and their fight is making it freakin' hard to plan your weekends. As the neutral (but annoyed) friend, you:**

A Remind each one how fun it was when you guys all went out together, then try to arrange a time for them to talk—with you as mediator.

B Can't help flipping out and yelling, "Get over your stupid argument already! You guys are ruining my social life!"

C Stay completely out of it. Nothing would be worse than getting caught in the cross fire.

2 It's two a.m. and you're just about to print out your ten-page English paper (due tomor—er, today) when your printer makes a weird noise and dies. Your plan of action?

A Try to stay calm, and e-mail your paper to all your friends, hoping one of them is awake and can print it for you. Backup plan? Text them so they see your request when they wake up in the morning.

B Kick the useless piece-of-crap printer across the room, start screaming, "Oh my god, this is *not* happening! I'm going to *fail*!", and wake up your entire family.

C Go straight to sleep—you're too tired to deal with it right now.

3 You just heard from the school gossip that your crush, who you've been exchanging witty banter with for the past two weeks, is in love with another girl. The first thing you do is:

A Figure the source might not be the most credible. You'll probably ask around and pay attention to see if he acts the same as usual around you.

B Go home and bawl and write in your journal. Then text everyone you know to try to find out who the mystery girl is so you can sabotage her.

C Act distant when you see him.

4 You're waiting tables and you drop a giant tray of full plates and glasses just as they were about to be some family's dinner. You immediately:

A Give the family a heartfelt apology, tell them you'll replace their orders with a rush on them, and ask the manager if you can give them a discount on their dinner.

B Turn beet red as you feel tears well up in your eyes, then start the waterworks.

C Run into the kitchen and quit on the spot.

5] Your parents tell you not to see a certain friend because they're worried she's a bad influence. Your reaction?

A You sit them down and rationally explain that if you comply with all their rules, there's no reason you should have to cut that friend out of your life.

B You start crying and screaming that they're horrible parents who are making you miserable, then stomp up to your room while threatening to run away.

C You say okay and keep seeing the friend anyway.

✳ [Mostly As] Cool connoisseur.

Your Zen-ish vibe is like butter on bread—smooth, and you spread it around! You're a pro at staying calm in even the most drama-inducing scenarios, which is a great habit to keep up throughout your life. Realizing that you need to deal with a situation head-on but never losing your cool about it will not only keep your heart rate from going up, but it will make

> Your Zen-ish vibe is like butter on bread.

people want to be around you. Like those two on-again friends of yours. Right on!

[Mostly Bs] Meltdown master.

Every time there's a minor snag, you're guaranteed to freak out. You get worried so easily that someone who doesn't know you would think the world was ending if they witnessed one of your meltdowns. It's easy to get all wrapped up in a situation (especially if it affects your social life), but for the sake of your sanity and that of your friends and fam, try to not let every little thing make you panic. Every time you freak out during the course of a week, write down what happened and how you reacted. At the end of the week, look over your list. Those situations weren't all heart-attack worthy, were they? Didn't think so! But seeing that on paper will help you stay calm next time a similar scenario pops up. Cool trick, huh?

> Someone who didn't know you would think the world was ending.

[Mostly Cs] Damsel in denial.

When something's stressing you out, you try your hardest to pretend nothing's wrong. It's normal to want to bypass drama, but instead of just going away, that drama usually ends up hitting you even harder later on (like, your parents will eventually realize you're still seeing the problem friend and punish you even worse!). Or you'll just internalize the stress, making your life way more

> You try your hardest to pretend nothing's wrong.

difficult and even compromising your health. Next time, instead of dodging a dramatic situation, take a breath and think about the best way to deal with it now, in the moment, step by step.

inner life

How independent are you?

Find out if you feel better flying solo or backed by a posse.

1) **You're planning on going to a party Friday night thrown by this girl you know from work. Who are you going with?**

a) Yourself. None of your best friends really know her, but you're pretty sure you'll know some people there.

b) One of your best girlfriends, if she wants to go. It'll be fun for her to get to know your work friend.

c) All your girls. Hello, you don't want people to think you don't have friends!

2) Your history midterm's coming up, and you've got a week to master Western civilization. What's your study tactic?

a) Crack the books and go over your notes solo. You just learn better that way.

b) Study by yourself most of the time, but reserve one or two nights to study with a group, just in case they have something in their notes that you missed.

c) Go to a different study group each night you can. You can't learn unless someone's quizzing you with flashcards.

3) When you get to college, do you think you'll rush a sorority?

a) No way! Just the thought of being around all those girls all the time gives you a headache.

b) You don't think so, at least not at first. You're excited to see who you can meet on your own before joining a group of insta-friends.

c) Absolutely! You love the thought of having such a supportive group of friends, especially in a new environment.

4) Out of nowhere, your boss at the ice cream shop starts insisting that all the employees wear these ridiculous upside-down-ice-cream-cone hats. What do you do?

a) Um, quit? There's no way you're going to sacrifice your individuality like that (not to mention be humiliated every day!).

b) Ask everyone you work with if they'd be willing to sign a petition against the new hats. If enough people band together against them, you might have a shot at staying cone-free.

c) Wear the hat. If everyone you work with has to wear it, it might foster a nice sense of togetherness.

5) You think the new girl in your math class is actually kind of cool (you totally bonded over your teacher's predictable "pop" quizzes), but at lunch you hear some of your friends verbally shredding her quirky clothes. You say:

a) "Last I checked, being an individual was a good thing. And anyway, her vintage tops kick Abercrombie's butt."

b) "I don't know. . . . She seems okay, but I really don't know her that well yet."

c) Nothing—and get up to grab another soda.

Mostly As Miss Independent.

You march to the beat of those cool bongos you found at a random garage sale last year. You don't need other people's opinions to help you make decisions in your life. In fact, you enjoy going against what others think and doing your own thing. It's awesome that you're so indie minded, and others secretly envy your courage to stand out. But make sure you don't give off the impression that you're above everyone else just because you don't feel the need to fit in with them. And let your real friends know that even if you don't agree with everything they say, their opinions really do matter to you.

Mostly Bs Posse optional.

When it comes to being independent, you've found a good balance in your life. You enjoy feeling like you've got a supportive group in your corner, but you sometimes listen to your inner voice anyway. And you know when to fly solo and when to gather your flock of friends for a group outing. Your friends' opinions matter to you, but you never blindly follow them, which shows that you know who you are and you're comfortable with it. And that's a pretty sweet quality to have!

Mostly Cs Team player.

You feel more comfortable when you're with your friends, whether you're going to a party or studying for a test. You crave the stability of knowing you won't have to brave new situations solo. While it's great to have a supportive posse you can count on, constantly relying on them (or just following the pack) can hold you back from discovering more about yourself without a bunch of other people's opinions swaying you. Try giving your independent side some more play. You can take baby steps at first. Join a group your friends aren't in, so you can meet new people, or study at a coffee shop alone. Before you know it, you'll feel stronger about who you are, without having to sacrifice your friends.

fun life

What's your **BAND** role?

Even if you're not aspiring to a life of groupies and touring, let's see how you'd be rocking that stage!

1 **When your parents brag to their friends about how creative you were as a kid, they always tell the story about how:**

A | Your self-styled song-and-dance routine would get a standing ovation every time you visited your dad's office.

B | You'd ask the deepest questions, like a mini-philosopher.

C | You'd never color inside the lines . . . or keep crayon off the walls!

2 When you have to get up in front of a group (like for a class project or performance), which of these colors are you most likely to wear?

A Red.

B Black.

C Orange.

3 At a party, you're usually the one:

A In the middle of a crowd, telling a joke everyone wants to hear.

B Hanging back and people watching.

C Making the rounds from group to group, talking to each one for a bit, then moving on.

4 In your group of friends, you're the one who always:

A Picks what the group will do on the weekends.

B Listens to everyone's problems and doles out advice.

C | Surprises everyone by pulling crazy stunts or talking to random people when you're out.

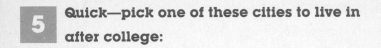

5 Quick—pick one of these cities to live in after college:

A | Los Angeles—Hollywood, here you come!

B | New York City—it's so cool and artsy.

C | Austin, Texas—or any other city that seems laid-back.

MOSTLY As: Lead singer/guitarist.

You were born to rock out in the spotlight. Like a lead singer or guitarist, who often writes the band's music, you thrive on calling the shots, whether you're picking a party for your friends to go to or throwing one of your own. Outgoing and endlessly energetic, you get a secret rush when all eyes are on you—and with your notice-me outfits and contagious laugh, they often are! You've got the whole stage-presence thing down!

MOSTLY Bs: Bass player.

Your quiet intensity would make you an awesome bass player. You've always been thoughtful and deep, and quite frankly, you'd rather express yourself by writing in your journal than entertaining a crowd. Sensitive and insightful, you love observing others and paying attention to the hidden details most people don't pick up on (kind of like how a really good bass line can be undetectable if you're not listening for it!).

MOSTLY Cs: Drummer.

You know the saying "She marches to the beat of her own drum"? That's totally you! You tend to keep people on their toes with your spontaneous antics and fun, offbeat energy. And you're always juggling a bunch of stuff at once, which is a handy skill for drummers, who have all those drums, snares, and cymbals in front of them. You often can't help going off on tangents, but your unpredictability is precisely the reason people love you!

5

Are you too **picky**?

Find out if your taste in guys is holding you back from finding one who's perfect for you!

1 You're at a party and spot a cute guy you've never seen before checking you out. Your first instinct is to:

A Go right up to him and start chatting. What've you got to lose? He thinks you're cute too, so you're sure you guys will hit it off.

B Hang back and see who he's there with before talking to him. You want to make sure he seems cool and isn't weird.

C Check out his band T-shirt. If it's not music you're into, then you know you won't even waste your time on him.

2 Your friend keeps saying you'd be perfect for her cousin Jake, who lives a town away. When she offers to set you guys up, you say:

A "Wouldn't it be romantic if we got married one day? When's our first date?"

B "Maybe. . . . Tell me what he's like."

C "Wait, what's wrong with him?"

3 For you to hit it off with a guy, he'd need to:

A Be cute and think you're awesome.

B Make you laugh and have a few things in common with you, like a love of basketball.

C Meet at least fourteen out of seventeen items on your list of criteria for your perfect guy, including height, age, and familiarity with the lyrics to all your favorite songs.

4 Your friends would probably describe your type as:

A Nonexistent. You don't have a type—you give 'em all a chance!

B Indie, sporty, or some other pretty general characteristic that could apply to a lot of guys.

C A figment of your imagination. A guy *that* perfect simply doesn't exist.

5 You've been IMing for a couple of days with a guy you met through friends, and he just asked you out for a burger. You think:

A "That's so sweet of him to ask me out for dinner! What a gentleman."

B "Maybe we should talk on the phone a few times first. If we don't run out of stuff to talk about, then I'll go."

C "He's not a vegetarian like me? Ugh, there's no chance we'll get along!"

Mostly As: Type? What type?

It's great that you're so open to different kinds of people, but by not being choosy at all, you may be preventing yourself from figuring out what qualities you're truly drawn to in a guy—and weeding out the losers. It's fun when a guy shows he's interested in you, but that doesn't necessarily mean he's *good* for you. Next time you really like someone, think about what makes you guys a good match. Being a little picky not only helps you find better guys for you, but it also teaches you about yourself in the process!

Mostly Bs: Type-specific.

You've got a great sense of what qualities you like in a guy, but you're not afraid to give someone who's different than your usual crushes a chance. Not only does that perspective help you meet guys you have a good chance of connecting with, but it makes you seem like more of a challenge to guys who might be interested in you. They know they have to work to get—and hold—your attention. Which actually makes you seem *more* interesting. And that's a cycle worth sticking with.

Mostly Cs: Total typecaster.

It's one thing to set high standards for who you want to date, but it's another to set them impossibly high, surround them with barbed wire, and set a fifty-character, case-sensitive password for it. Knowing what you like and what you're about is awesome, but when you apply your exclusive tastes to people, you're probably keeping yourself from meeting someone great. So next time you meet someone who seems cool but hasn't heard of that obscure band you're obsessed with, don't write him off. Who knows, maybe he can introduce you to your next obsession-worthy band.

6

What makes people **JEALOUS** of you?

We all have qualities other people only *wish* they had. Find out which of yours are coveted commodities.

1] **It's Wednesday night and you don't have weekend plans locked down yet. So you:**

A Coordinate a karaoke night on Saturday for all your friends (and their crushes)!

B Decide to go see a band that you've heard good things about. If some friends want to go with you, that'd be great, but if not, that's cool too.

C Figure you'll use the time to get cracking on your college essays—who cares if you don't have to finish them till next year!

2 You meet a cute new guy at a party and he comes over to chat. How do you judge if he's someone you might want to date?

A If he's easygoing enough to get along with all your friends.

B If he loves all the same books or TV shows you do and shares your weird sense of humor.

C If he seems as focused as you are on doing well in school and getting into a great college.

3 The best compliment someone could give you is:

A "You're so much fun to be around."

B "You don't care what people think of you."

C "You're going to be a huge success someday."

4] It's the beginning of the school year, when everyone's signing up for extracurricular clubs at school. You might sign up for:

A Cheerleading, drama club, student council, peer counseling—there are so many, you can't decide!

B Probably nothing. You're not so into joining stuff, and the clubs at school are especially cheesy.

C Only the clubs that you think will look great on your college apps and guarantee you an officer position.

5] Your friend is going through a bout of seriously low self-esteem. She's convinced she looks gross and no one likes her. You help cheer her up by:

A Making sure she looks her hottest and taking her out to a club where she can have fun and flirt with tons of guys.

B Reminding her of the things that are unique about her. Like if she's an artist, you bring out her sketches and tell her how great they are.

C Sitting down with her and making a list of all the things she doubts about herself and what actions she can take that will make her feel better about each one.

[Mostly As] Your outgoing nature.

When people think of you, they think "social butterfly." You're friends with people in all different groups, and you're never at a loss for weekend plans. People see how easy making friends is for you and wish they had the fun, outgoing vibe you emanate. Use your fine-tuned social skills to reach out to kids at school who may have a harder time bonding with people. Not only will it help them feel included, but it'll make you feel like your party-girl personality is being used to do some good in the world.

You're friends with people in all different groups.

[Mostly Bs] Your independent spirit.

People envy your ability to do your own thing. You know who you are, and you're comfortable enough in your own skin to disregard anyone who may not understand you. People respect the fact that you have a defined set of tastes and interests, like in the music you listen to and the clothes you wear, and they see you as cool and alternative because you never feel the need to conform to the masses. Only thing is, you can seem a little standoffish to those who don't know you. Even though you're not a joiner, maybe a fun, different club would actually be worth your while. Who knows, you might meet some people who share your edge but can introduce you to some great new interests.

> They see you as cool and alternative.

[Mostly Cs] Your driven demeanor.

Most likely to succeed, anyone? Your ambitious nature makes others wish they had their future all planned out like you do. You know what you want out of life, and you're already taking the steps to ensure that you get there—at an impressively young age, at that!

You know what you want out of life.

Not that you don't have fun, but most of your energy goes to making sure you get into a good college and are well on your way to having the career you want. Sometimes your remarkable drive can make friends feel less than successful. But as long as you keep spreading the wealth and helping your friends see *their* strengths, you'll be able to manage your social and professional lives like a pro.

7

Are you a **go-getter**?

Find out if you're driving on the road to success or just enjoying the ride.

1) **When it comes to deciding which colleges you'll apply to, you:**

a) Have already researched your top twenty choices, cross-referenced them by academics and campus life, and started on your application essays.

b) Have looked into a couple of schools online, but you still have a little while until you have to make a decision.

c) Haven't really thought about it. You'll handle all that senior year.

2) Summer's coming. What are you planning on doing to while away the days?

a) Finding an internship and taking a few intensive courses at a local college. What better time to get a head start on your career than while everyone else is wasting time at the pool?

b) Getting a summer job, doing your summer reading, and hanging out with your friends.

c) Absolutely nothing! That's what summer's for!

3) For you to really hit it off with a guy, he'd definitely have to show which of the following qualities?

a) Ambition that matches yours. A slacker just wouldn't understand that you're busy with studying and extracurriculars and can't spend all your time hanging out with him.

b) The ability to make you laugh, and at least a couple of interests in common so you guys can connect on an intellectual level.

(c) He'd have to be cute and be fun at parties.

4) **If your friends had to pick three words to describe you, which of these would they most likely pick?**

a) Driven, focused, ambitious.

b) Hardworking, fun, even-keeled.

c) Laid-back, carefree, relaxed.

5) **Your bio teacher just made the class clown your lab partner for the semester. Your first thought:**

a) "Great, how am I supposed to get an A with that joker bringing me down? Maybe I can request a new partner."

b) "I might have to work a little harder, but at least I'll have fun all semester . . . and who knows, maybe he'll surprise me by being a science whiz."

c) "Cool . . . now I'll have someone to joke around and goof off with."

✳ One-track wonder.

No one would ever accuse you of slacking! It seems like ever since you were born, everything you've done has been for the purpose of getting into your dream college and succeeding at your dream career. You've always

> You don't want to burn out before you even get to college.

aimed superhigh and achieved your goals, and you have no intention of stopping now. Being goal oriented is great, but when you put all your energy in your ideal future, you're depriving yourself of living in—and enjoying—the present. And you may be giving people around you the idea that you're too busy trying to succeed to care about them. Try going out with friends more, or joining a club that has nothing to do with your future major. You don't want to burn out before you even get to college, so balancing work and play will do you good.

Confident contender.

Your friends are right in thinking you're even-keeled. People could learn from your ability to live life to the fullest, socially *and* academically, and not feel the need to push anyone else down to do it. You know when to stay in and study and when to go out and have fun—and parents, teachers, and other adults are always saying how poised you are. Your winning combination of fun and ambition will not only take you far in school, but it'll put you on the path to success in the rest of your life. Nice!

> Your friends are right in thinking you're even-keeled.

Mostly Cs Slacker girl.

Your motto channels Bob Marley: "Everything's gonna be all right!" You see no reason to get worked up about grades, college, or anything else to do with the future. But even though

37

everything probably will be okay, things will turn out a whole lot better than okay if you take control of your life instead of just letting it happen to you. The good news is that being so laid-back can work to your advantage, making you stand out from all the cookie-cutter overachievers applying to the same college you are. But you have to *make* it work for you. Try joining some clubs you think might be fun. When you actually *like* doing something, chances are you'll excel at it, and impress!

You see no reason to get worked up about grades.

What MOVIE-THEATER SNACK are you?

When the lights dim and the trailers start, treats are a necessity!

 What school club appeals to you most?

A | Cheerleading.

B | Debate club.

(C) | School clubs aren't really your thing.

2 **Pick some shoes, any shoes:**

A | Ballet flats.

(B) | Wedges or heels.

C | Doc Martens that you've doodled on.

3 **Which of these nicknames would your friends most likely call you?**

A | The girl next door.

B | Ms. Well-rounded.

C | Rebel girl.

4 **Your ideal vacation:**

A | Sightseeing in Paris.

B | Exploring, then partying, in London.

C | Trekking through the jungles of Africa.

5 **Which life goal is most important to you?**

A | Falling in love.

B | Having it all.

C | Making it on your own terms.

MOSTLY As: Popcorn.

Popcorn is a wholesome classic everyone loves, just like you. Traditional and a true romantic, you adore all the big-screen ideals, like true love (admit it, you're a sucker for a heartwarming ending) and the good guys beating the bad guys in the end (ah, justice!). Just make sure you mix it up every now and then (maybe throw in a few Milk Duds?) so no one will think you've gone stale.

MOSTLY Bs: Sour Patch Kids.

Like this mouthwatering treat, you're exceptionally well balanced. You can be a sweetheart, but your friends know they can count on you to speak the truth, even if it's a bit tart. You know how to have fun but can switch to your serious, focused mode on a moment's notice. And since you've got such a wide range of interests (sweet, tart, and everything in between), there's nothing you can't sink your teeth into and conquer.

MOSTLY Cs: Smuggled-in fast food.

You live on the edge, and you wouldn't have it any other way! You've never been just a member of the pack (or had the patience to wait in line at the concession stand!), and people are naturally drawn to your unique ideas and risk-loving boldness. You'd rather follow your own rules, not your parents' or school's—or, uh, the movie theater's!

9

What makes you **HOT** to guys?

When guys say a girl's hot, they don't just mean her looks. Every girl has a secret seductive quality that draws guys to her. Find out what makes you irresistible!

1 You're hanging out with your friends at the mall when you see the cute guy in your history class checking out sneakers. You:

A Tell your friends to be quiet while you sneak up behind him and loudly blurt out, "Excuse me, sir, do you work here? Can you help me find some shoes?"

B Wait till he sees you and says hi, then ask what he thought of the pop quiz you guys had on Friday.

C Point to the shoes he's looking at and say, "Those are cool, but the gray ones over there are totally you—you should get 'em!"

2 You're in home ec, and in front of the whole class, your teacher, Mr. Dern, totally insults the (lopsided) pillow you sewed. You can feel yourself turning fire-engine red, but you think fast and say:

A "You're right, Mr. Dern—I hate my pillow! I wish it was never sewn!" as you dramatically throw it across the room.

B "Um, but don't you think the imperfections make it that much more lovable?"

C "How do you know the person I made it for doesn't have a lopsided head? You shouldn't judge before you know all the facts!"

3 You're finally going out with the guy you've been crushing on forever. Your perfect date would consist of:

A Surprising him by taking him to play paintball— then totally kicking his butt!

B Seeing a romantic comedy and holding hands as you share an extralarge popcorn.

C Seeing a documentary you're both excited about and then grabbing a late-night latte as you discuss the best parts of the movie.

4 If you were in a dating slump, your friends would most likely try to lift your spirits by telling you:

A "What guy wouldn't want you? You're so cute and funny!"

B "What guy wouldn't want you? You're so cute and caring!"

C "What guy wouldn't want you? You're so cute and smart!"

5 You're going to a party Friday that you know your crush will be at, and you've planned the perfect outfit:

A A shirt that says "You lookin' at me?" with a cutoff miniskirt and colorful leggings.

B A dress with a pretty detail, like ruffles, and dainty ballet flats.

C Your favorite band T-shirt (you happen to know he's into that band too) with Converse high-tops and jeans that make your butt look amazing.

Mostly As: You're the fun girl.

You're the girl guys say is "frickin' hilarious!" You have a knack for being spontaneous, which guys are instinctively drawn to, and you're never at a loss for what to say to keep them cracking up. You have a talent for always being the life of the party, even when you're not *at* a party. But if you're interested in dating a guy and not just making him laugh, try bringing up some more serious stuff too. That way he'll realize you're about more than just getting a few giggles.

Mostly Bs: You're the sweet girl.

Guys are drawn to your sensitive, feminine nature because it smooths out their rough edges. They feel like they can really open up to you and their secrets will always be safe. You're the girl guys can't wait to bring home to meet their mom, because they know your nurturing quality will come shining through—making you seem like the perfect girlfriend. Being sweet is great, but make sure you're not afraid to speak up about your *own* needs and opinions.

Mostly Cs: You're the witty girl.

You've got this way of making guys feel like you really "get" them, which they find superattractive. Guys are drawn to the challenge of getting a girl as smart as you to fall for them. Not one to play dumb, you've got cool interests and know how to keep a conversation going by bouncing back those lightning-quick one-liners, so guys never feel like they need to strain for stuff to talk about. Next time you like a guy, make a point of really listening to what he's saying, so he doesn't feel like when he's talking, you're just planning your next witty comeback.

social life

Are you a **good friend**?

You love your girlfriends, but do you always *show* it?

1] One of your friends just got into a huge fight with her boyfriend and is freaking out that he might break up with her. When she calls you bawling, you:

(A) Drop everything you're doing and meet her wherever she is.

(B) Stay on the phone with her until she calms down and get her to explain what happened, then offer your opinion on what she should do next.

(C) Roll your eyes and tell her things will be fine. You're tired of hearing about her relationship dramas.

2 You're at the mall with your best friend and you both spot the same awesome dress in a store window. When you're deciding who's got dibs on it, you:

A Just let her have it. It'll make her happy, and there are plenty of other dresses out there for you.

B Tell her you can both get it and wear it on different days—either that or you'll just have to flip for it.

C Insist you saw it first. Then remind her of all the cute things she has that you don't.

3 Your friend is not doing *bien* in Spanish class and asks if you can come over and help her study the night before your big test. Knowing that you study better on your own, you:

A Are happy to spend hours tutoring her anyway.

B Let her know you need to study by yourself first, give her copies of your meticulous notes, and agree to quiz her over the phone later on.

C Make up an excuse to get out of it. Why should *your* grade suffer to better hers?

4 You hear a loud thump behind you and turn to see that your best friend just fell down on the stairs between classes, dropping all her stuff. The next bell is about to ring, and you're supposed to be in third period. What do you do?

A Stay with her and help her pick up her stuff, then take her to the nurse's office even if she says she's okay. The heck with class . . . your friend is hurt!

B Help her gather her stuff while saying, "Nothing to see here!" to ward off the gawkers. When you're sure she's okay, you go to your class.

C Jet to class, yelling, "Sorry, I've got a quiz!" She'll understand.

5 While your friend is out of town, her boyfriend makes a move on you. When she gets back, you:

A Pretend nothing happened and do your best to avoid him. She'll see his true colors when the time is right.

B Wait to see if he does it again (just in case it was a fluke). If he does, you'll sit her down and tell her.

C Say nothing, but keep flirting with him. It feels so forbidden and fun!

[Mostly As]
Yes—you give it all you've got.

If you were a religious figure, you'd be the patron saint of friendship. You never fail to put your friends first, even if it means making some sacrifices. Your devotion is commendable, but if you always push your own needs to the side, you risk losing your sense of self. Plus, always giving and never asking for anything in return could be telling your friends you don't mind being taken for granted. Put yourself first sometimes, and don't hesitate to ask your friends for help when you need it. You've been such a generous pal to them, they'll be more than happy to oblige.

[Mostly Bs]
Yes—you tell it like it is.

Your friends know you have great common sense, and they always come to you when they need solid, down-to-earth advice. They appreciate the fact that most of the time, you're honest with them without being harsh. While being honest is almost always the way to go, there can be times when keeping mum is the better policy. When you're about to tell your friend something she may not like, consider how you would feel in her shoes. If the honesty would upset you more than help you, keep it to yourself.

[Mostly Cs]
Maybe—you tend to put yourself first.

The best friendships are equal parts give and take, but you seem to have only mastered that last part. Yes, your friends should know that everyone has to look out for number one, but you need to realize when a little sacrifice for friendship's sake is worth more than a dress in a window or some flirt sessions with a guy. Because if you don't, your friends will catch on that your relationship is one-sided and want out. When you make a friend's day or help her through a rough patch, not only does she feel good, but you will as well (bonus!). Try being a bit more giving and you'll form a stronger bond.

11

What **STRENGTH** sets you apart?

You're the superhero of your own life! Find out what your hidden power is.

1) **Your English teacher assigned you to a group project about the Shakespeare play you're reading. You're the group member who:**

a) Gets everyone to agree on a topic and volunteers to present your project in front of the class.

b) Makes sure everyone feels like they have a say in the project and hosts the meetings at your house.

c) Makes an outline for the project and figures out how all the elements need to come together.

d) Writes a clever skit or creates the visual aids for your project.

2) **If you could have your pick of dream internships this summer, who would you work with?**

a) A successful CEO—it's fascinating how one person's leadership abilities make an entire company work.

b) A social worker who rescues kids from abusive homes and helps place them into loving ones.

c) A movie producer—you want to see how they juggle so many elements to make a film happen.

d) A fashion designer—you're interested in the creative process behind a line of clothes.

3) **You have a crush on this guy who you're pretty sure likes you too. Besides just flirting, what strategy do you use to get him to fall for you?**

a) You throw a party at a local hangout, inviting all your friends and his friends, so you'll have a chance to talk to him outside of school.

b) You always make sure to be there when he needs someone to vent to about his ridiculously hard test or family issues.

c) You figure out all his favorite bands and places to hang out, so you can just "happen" to show up at the same concerts or restaurants.

d) You create a series of "secret admirer" stickers with your doodles on them and leave one in his locker each week with a clue to who you are. Pretty soon, you'll let him figure it out.

4) Your parents tell you they have some bad news about this year's family vacation. The most horrible, nightmarish thing they could say to you is that:

a) You no longer have a say in any of the activities you'll do.

b) They're going back on their promise to let you bring your best friend.

c) They picked your little brother's cheesy theme park suggestion over your proposed tour of a big city's cultural hot spots.

d) You're not allowed to bring your iPod or sketch pad.

5) The application to your top-choice college gives you four options of phrases to begin your essay with. Which do you pick?

a) I knew I had to take charge when . . .

b) I knew I had to help them when . . .

c) I knew I had to think fast when . . .

d) I knew I had to create something amazing when . . .

Mostly As   Your ability to lead.

Whether your friends are trying to figure out what to do this weekend or your group in class needs a project leader, you're the girl they turn to. You have this amazing ability to get people behind your cause and make them truly excited about it. You thrive when you feel like you're in charge, and you know how to work around any obstacles. Whether you set out to become a powerful politician or a successful CEO, you'll achieve your goal. Just make sure the people around you feel that their opinions matter too. A truly great leader makes her team believe they're all working together toward something they can all be proud of.

Mostly Bs — Your insight into people.

People feel safe and cared for when they're around you, because you have a great gift for figuring out what others need (even when they don't say it out loud) and then making them feel better. Your friends probably joke that you're the "mom" of the group, and they may be on to something. You've always been more mature than most kids your age, and you feel good when you've got a situation under control. The way you can read people and know how to help them— and your knack for staying collected in any situation—makes people gravitate toward you, and you wouldn't have it any other way. Just make sure the ones you're caring for are giving you the same TLC you're giving them!

Mostly Cs Your sharp mind.

You're what people call a mastermind. You love learning, and you use all that knowledge you collect to think fast in tricky situations. People are amazed at your ability to come up with smart solutions to potential problems in no time, which is why everyone wants to be your partner on class projects and all your friends come to you for honest advice. Because you're so innovative, you probably come up with a million ideas a minute, but take the time to really focus on a couple of your brightest ones. Before you know it, you'll be on your way to accomplishing something great, like creating a useful new Web site for the kids at your school or doing whatever else you put your mind to.

Your creativity.

People always describe you as daring and unconventional, and you know what? They're right. You have the soul of an artist, and the talent of one as well. You have the ability to think outside the box and make something unexpected out of something ordinary, like the time you made your old jeans into a one-of-a-kind bag. That innovative vibe draws people to you, and you're seen as the hipster in your group of friends. Sometimes, though, people see you as the artist/slacker, not the high achiever. To prove them wrong and reach your sky-high potential, think about how your creations can really work in the world (maybe you start making more denim bags and selling them around town). Once you let others see what you're capable of, there's no limit to where your talent can take you.

fun life

Who's your
COMIC-BOOK HERO?

You totally don't *need* a hero (you're your own!),
but let's just say you have a date with a guy in
spandex who likes to save the world. . . .

 When you meet a cute new guy, the thing that always wins you over is:

A | His hot muscles.

B | His ability to trade witty banter with you.

C | His sensitivity.

 The gift you'd most love from your guy is:

A | A beautiful necklace with a precious stone.

B | A first-edition book from your absolute favorite author.

C | A portrait he's drawn of you or a song he's written about you.

 3 **You crush on guys who:**

A | Seem strong and have it together.

B | Are quirky and challenge you intellectually.

C | Are deep and moody, like artists or musicians.

4 **You won a new car! You would most love to get:**

A | A powerful Porsche.

B | An environment-helping hybrid.

C | A sleek and alluring Jaguar.

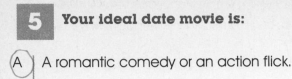

5 Your ideal date movie is:

A) A romantic comedy or an action flick.

B | A documentary or a foreign film.

C | An intense drama or a black comedy.

MOSTLY As: Superman.

You love a classic, athletic guy who knows just what to do in any situation, like Superman. Strong, silent guys who aren't afraid to show their mushy side appeal to you too. People would probably call you a girly girl, but that doesn't mean you're a damsel in distress—you've been known to get your hands dirty and work up a good sweat.

MOSTLY Bs: Spider-Man.

Your superhero needs to have smarts to match yours, so Spider-Man's your guy. Peter Parker was a brain before he morphed into Spidey, so you two would never be at a loss for compelling stuff to talk about. You're drawn to witty guys who not only are cute but also can stimulate your mind by making you laugh while making you think!

MOSTLY Cs: Batman.

You like dark and edgy guys, and it doesn't get much darker than Batman's Batcave! There's just something appealing to you about a way artistic guy who's in touch with his sensitive side, even if he's something of a bad boy. You can't help it—that brooding, tortured soul thing gets you every time!

13

Is he shady?

He may seem sincere, but there are ways to tell if your guy has nothing to hide or if he's just plain shady.

1 **He was supposed to meet you at the mall at two, but when the clock hit two, he was nowhere to be found. Instead, he:**

A Called to say he was running late because he had to drop his little brother off at a friend's, but got there at two-twenty like he said he would.

B Got there at two-twenty and apologized a few times for being late but never gave you a reason.

C Was MIA until you called him at two-twenty and then muttered that he was out late last night and slept in.

2 He gets a text message when you're with him and you see that it's from a girl you don't know. When you bring up her name, he:

A Tells you it's his cousin—and come to think of it, you do remember him mentioning her a while back.

B Tells you it's his cousin—but you don't remember him ever talking about her before.

C Defensively snaps, "It's just a friend, stop spying on me!"

3 You guys are out to dinner one-on-one when a friend of yours (who he only sort-of knows) sees you and comes over to say hi. What does he do?

A Gives her a hug and invites her to sit down and share dessert.

B Says hi but then just sits there checking his voice mail while you and she finish chatting.

C Mumbles hey but immediately gets up to go to the bathroom and stays there until she's gone.

4 **He introduces you as his girlfriend:**

A Whenever you meet his friends, his mom, basically anyone he's close to.

B Once in a while, but he usually just says, "This is [your name]."

C Yeah, he never has.

5 **Before he started dating you, he had a reputation as:**

A A one-girl guy. He's had girlfriends, but you've never heard of any drama in his past.

B Someone who dated around, but not a ton.

C A total player.

Mostly As: True blue.

Sounds like your guy's got nothing to hide. If he can't be somewhere to meet you, he tells you why. If he bumps into a friend of yours, he's sweet to her instead of bolting. And you know pretty much everything about his romantic past. In fact, he's so honest, it can be tempting to take that openness for granted. But don't, so he realizes it's something you actually value. Next time he introduces you to someone, say, "It's so considerate that you always remember to introduce me." That way he knows it means a lot to you. Oh, and don't forget to return the favor by being just as honest with him!

Mostly Bs: Partly cloudy.

Your guy does some things that make you go, "Hmm," but he's not necessarily being shady. If you haven't been going out that long, you may just not know him well enough to read him perfectly. And if he hasn't had much relationship experience, he may not realize that some of his actions make you wonder. But it does sound as though he's at least *trying* to be a good boyfriend. So help him out. Next time he does something that sets off your shady detector, ask him about it in a curious—not confrontational—way. Confrontation can make a guy nervous—and nerves can actually make him act shady when he doesn't really mean to!

Mostly Cs: Gloomy forecast.

Sorry to say it, but you probably already suspected: your guy's quite the shady character. It's not a definite that he's hiding something you'd be upset to find out, but he's sure acting like it. And that's a sign he doesn't respect you enough to be up-front. His rep's got shady written all over it, and without a ton of maturing, his sneakiness and defensiveness will be hard habits to break. The longer you stay with him, the worse you'll feel. You may even start making excuses for his warped actions, or worse, start thinking you deserve to be treated this way. So break it off with him now. When you meet other, nonshady guys in the future, you'll wonder what you were ever doing with this jerk. Promise.

14

Are you too **predictable**?

Find out if people can't wait to see what you'll do next—or already know your next move before you make it.

1] **When it comes to changing up your style, you:**

A Are a total chameleon. You have to change your hair color at least once a month or you get painfully bored!

B Are always evolving. Like if you spot a cool new Victorian fashion trend, you'll introduce some brocade and ruffles into your wardrobe.

C Don't do it that often. In fact, you've had the same basic look since sixth grade.

2] **A typical Friday night for you means:**

A Who knows? Every week, you seem to do something completely different with a new group of people.

B Just cruising around town with your friends until you guys decide what to do. But if you find out where your crush is going to be, you're totally there.

C Hanging out with your friends and watching DVDs.

3] **You're bored with ski club and environmental club, so you:**

A Start karate classes with a private instructor and take up photography on the side.

B Drop out of one of them and sign up for the literary journal at school instead.

C Figure you'll stick them out. If you still feel bored by the end of the year, you'll pick something new next year.

4 You totally hit it off with a jock, but you usually go for more artsy types. Your best friend would probably say:

A "You won't stop till you date every type, will you?"

B "Hmmm . . . he's different for you. Can't wait to see what happens!"

C "Oh. My. God. I think hell has just frozen over!"

5 You're staying at your friend's house for dinner, and her mom puts a plate down in front of you with an Indian dish you've never even heard of before. You:

A Dig in. Anything exotic is good in your mind!

B Ask her mom what's in the dish, and try it to be polite.

C Push it around on your plate but don't taste it. You never eat anything if you're not sure of all the ingredients.

[Mostly As] Live wire.

Your friends are constantly waiting to see what unpredictable stuff you'll be up to next. One minute, you'll be shopping quietly at the mall, and the next, you're belting out the song that was stuck in your head at top lung capacity. "Boring" is the last word anyone would use to describe you, and you've come to like being known as the wild one. Just make sure you pull all those crazy antics because you want to, not because people around you expect you to. Keeping up any act, even a wacky one, can get exhausting!

[Mostly Bs] Mix master.

You're totally cool with breaking out of your comfort zone and doing something out of the ordinary, like switching up your look or ditching a club you're bored with, but you don't act crazy just for the sake of being offbeat. You have a desire for new experiences, but not a need for them, and people are naturally drawn to your fun, spontaneous self.

[Mostly Cs] Same drill sergeant.

People have come to count on your reliability. You're loyal to your tastes, and your friends know what to expect. It's tempting to stick to what you know works for you, but you might have a little more fun if you mix things up from time to time. It can get boring to eat the same foods and hang out with all the same people, so try a new dish or make a friend from a new crowd. Not only will the people around you see you in a surprising light, but you might experience something new that you won't believe you ever lived without!

15

Do you act your age?

Stuck in the good old days or acting old before your time? This quiz will reveal whether you're in a time warp.

1) **You're at your aunt's birthday dinner. After the meal, where can you be found?**

a) Playing with your little cousins. They've got this great energy that you love to be around.

b) Making a beeline for the bedroom so you can check your messages and texts in private. You put in your time mingling with the grown-ups, now it's back to your life.

c) Lingering at the table for tea with the adults. They always discuss the most interesting things, like politics.

2) **If you could land your dream job after college, you'd be:**

a) A toy tester for a huge toy manufacturer. You couldn't think of anything more fun.

b) Working in the fashion or entertainment industry. Those jobs seem so fast paced and creative.

c) Sitting in a corner office making important decisions while an assistant gets you coffee.

3) **You and a friend are thinking of seeing a movie tonight. After flipping through the listings, what do you suggest?**

a) A gross-out comedy. Nothing makes you laugh harder than fart jokes and kicks to someone's crotch!

b) A movie set in college. It's like your world, but with more drama!

c) An independent foreign film. Most Hollywood movies are so juvenile and dumb.

4) **What do you love most about your group of friends?**

a) Um, you're still giggling about that crazy dance you guys made up the other day.

b) They're loyal, fun, and great to gossip with!

c) They're ambitious, not immature like the other kids at school.

5) **Which do you most often hear from your parents?**

a) "Stop goofing around. You've got to start being *serious*."

b) "Get off the Internet. You've been plugged in to something all day."

c) "Lighten up a little. We're the parents and you're the kid."

Kidlike conduct.

You never understand why people take life so seriously. The way you see it, if you're not having fun, what's the point? You love goofing around, making gross jokes, and generally getting into mischief. People enjoy being around you since you're such a big kid at heart, but if you don't realize that there are situations when you need to act your age, you might be perceived as inappropriate (or worse, annoying!)—and it's no fun if you're the only one laughing. If you can inject your carefree youthfulness with a sense of responsibility, you'll find that life can be both fun *and* meaningful.

Mostly Bs Age-appropriate attitude.

You're sensible enough to set goals for yourself (like that fabulous job you're working toward), but you still love being young (you're not above some good gossip now and then). People are drawn to you because you live in the moment. You know when to goof off and when to tone it down. When it comes to acting your age, you're exactly where you should be.

Mostly Cs — Mature mentality.

You can't wait to be older, and if we're talking attitude, you're already going on thirty! You were done with youthful antics years ago, and your tastes have matured way earlier than most of your peers' (Slapstick comedies? Please!). It's understandable to want independence and intelligent conversations, but by living in the future, you're missing out on all the fun of being young (Come on—even your parents are telling you to lighten up!). So let loose and have some fun. You can still have grown-up interests while letting your inner kid come out to play!

16

What kind of GIRLFRIEND are you?

Everyone brings something different to a relationship. Find out *your* couple contribution.

1 You take your new guy out with your friends and it's a total disaster—he keeps putting his foot in his mouth. After you two leave the restaurant, you:

A Grab his hand and tell him you're sure your friends loved him.

B Immediately make a plan to all hang out again so your friends can get to know him when he's not so nervous.

C Can't stop laughing . . . it was like you were watching a sketch comedy show where everything that could've gone wrong did!

2 **Your guy had a horrible day. How do you cheer him up?**

A You bake him a batch of his favorite cookies, write "I love you" on them in frosting, and bring them over to his house.

B You listen while he tells you what's bothering him, then give him advice about how to turn things around.

C You tell him that story about your nephew that cracks him up every time.

3 **His friends tell him they wish they had a girlfriend like you because you're so:**

A Good to him.

B Down-to-earth.

C Hilarious.

4 **What holiday gift are you most likely to give him?**

A That new video game you know he's been eyeing.

B A watch . . . his broke and he needs a new one.

C A bunch of funny DVDs so you can watch them and crack up together.

5 **The conversations you have on your dates are usually about:**

A Who loves the other person more.

B School stuff, and your hopes and dreams.

C Wacky stories that happened to both of you.

> ### Mostly As: You're the sweet girlfriend.

You're a born giver, and your lucky boyfriend gets to savor your generosity. Understanding and forgiving, you make him feel truly loved and cared for, and you're a die-hard romantic, so there's never a shortage of lovey-doveyness when you're around. Just make sure he dotes on you as much as you dote on him!

Mostly Bs: You're the real girlfriend.

He loves you because you're so no-nonsense and honest. When it comes to your relationship, you're practical and never overreact over little things. And you make it a point to learn everything about your guy and connect with him on a deep level—in fact, you can often guess what he's going to say before he says it. You leave the cheesy, mushy stuff to others—for you, it's all about being yourselves around each other. Just don't forget to inject your relationship with a little romance— it's fun to be mushy now and then!

Mostly Cs: You're the funny girlfriend.

With you around, the good times just keep rolling. You're upbeat, fun to hang out with, and never take yourself too seriously. Your guy loves your up-for-anything spirit and the fact that he can joke around with you like with one of the guys. Just make sure you and your guy bond over mutual tastes and opinions, not just jokes. Even if you're laughing all the time, he needs to know you can take things seriously when it really counts.

17

Are you a RISK taker?

Go out on a limb and find out with this quiz.

1) **You and your boyfriend of eight months have a good, steady thing going, but you're weirdly drawn to the new guy in your art history class who makes thoughtful comments and amazing doodles on his notebooks. You:**

a) Start planning how you'll make Doodle Boy fall in love with you—or at least make out with you—by Homecoming. Who are you to defy love at first sight?

b) Engage in some friendly but not flirty banter with Doodle Boy. You're always open to making more cool friends.

c) Avoid Doodle Boy at all costs. If you guys hit it off . . . well, you'd rather not complicate your situation.

2) Your school invited your absolute favorite author to speak at an assembly. After she finishes (and you can actually breathe again), you:

a) March right up and shove the short story you're writing into her hands while begging her to critique it for you.

b) Have your teacher introduce you, then muster up the courage to tell her you love her work and if she ever needs a research assistant you'd be honored to help.

c) Circle her all night like a dog marking its territory but never utter a word . . . what if you say something moronic, or worse, spill punch on her shoes?

3) Tryouts for the fall play are in a week. You've only done stage crew, but for a while now, you've been secretly craving being in the spotlight, not operating it. You'll most likely:

a) Channel Audrey Hepburn and audition for the lead. What have you got to lose?

b) Try out for a supporting role. Being onstage but not center stage will be a good way to see if acting's really your thing.

c) Sign up for stage crew again. You've gotten really close with that group over the past year, and you *are* pretty good with a power saw.

4) You carpooled with a friend to a party where people are drinking, and it's already a little past your curfew. The parents will ground you for eternity if you don't get home pronto (and for even longer if they find out what the party's like). Your friend's ready to go and you can't tell if she's still tipsy. You:

a) Hop in the car. She says she's sober, and would never forgive you if you didn't go with her.

b) Take the time to find a ride with someone sober, then prepare to suffer some serious wrath from your parents for being late and from your friend for not going with her.

c) Call your parents to come pick you both up. You'd rather wind up grounded at home than injured in the hospital.

5) History is your favorite subject, and your teacher loves to incite class discussions. How often would you say you join in?

a) Let's just say you've almost lost your voice by the end of class on multiple occasions.

b) When you feel superpassionate about a point or are almost positive you know the right answer to a question.

c) Pretty much never. You're convinced you'll forget what you wanted to say and start babbling incoherently.

Mostly As   Danger-seeking.

Slow down there, Tony Hawk. You're not scared of much, and you'll try anything once, so taking risks whenever you get the chance is second nature to you. But living all-or-nothing all the time puts you in danger of crashing and burning. That's not to say you shouldn't challenge yourself. Some risks are awesome because they let you explore what you like and what you're good at (like trying out for the play). But others aren't worth their possible consequences, like taking a ride with someone who's been drinking or cheating on your boyfriend. If you take every risk that presents itself to you, good or bad, chances are that at least one will backfire. So before you try something potentially dangerous, think about whether the outcome is worth the risk itself.

Mostly Bs Risk-ready.

You have a pretty strong sense of who you are and what you stand for, which is why you're willing to dive into new and different situations without going off the deep end. You can tell a good risk from a bad one—and major props for all the times you've stayed true to yourself, even when tempted by people who don't! Since you've got such a good head on your shoulders, try sharing the wealth. If you know someone who constantly puts herself in harm's way by taking thoughtless risks, try reminding her of the possible real-life consequences. And if you have a friend who never puts herself out there, encourage her to be bolder. You just might get your biggest payoff yet.

Mostly Cs Proceeding with caution.

Hey, you there, lurking in the shadows of your braver self—come into the light! Yes, it can be totally scary to step out of your comfort zone, but it's impossible to know what you're capable of if you're too freaked out to try something new. You're probably anxious about what people will think of you if you speak up in class or audition for the play. But they'll probably think you're gutsy for going for it. Pick one thing that you've wanted to do but have been too scared to try, and break it up into minigoals. Like try out for a bit part first, and next time go for a bigger role. And prepare to say hello to your brand-new comfort zone.

18

Are BOYS taking over your brain?

It's fun to be a bit guy crazy, but when you're obsessed, it can be a problem!

1 Your perfect night out would be:

A Going to a party where most of the people don't go to your school. So many opportunities to flirt with new guys!

B Having dinner with a group of friends—and your crush.

C Having a sleepover with your girlfriends: videos, junk food, and tons of girl talk! What more do you need?

2 Whenever you go on vacation with your family, you make a point of:

A Sneaking away from your parents as often as possible to scout the hotel for cute guys. If you don't meet at least one guy to flirt with, you consider the whole trip a washout.

B Having fun with your family and looking cute on the beach. You never know who you'll set your blanket down next to.

C Relaxing incognito. It's nice to not have to care about your appearance for once. If you want to wear a big floppy hat and read a book under an umbrella, that's your right.

3 When you rejoin your friends in the stands after talking to a new guy during halftime at your school's homecoming game, they say:

A "Another entry for your list of crushes?"

B "He's hot! What'd you guys talk about?"

C "Oh my god, I can't believe you talked to a guy! Did anyone just see that cow flying?"

4 You're at the mall's food court with your friend when a cute guy sits down on the bench next to you. You:

A Turn away from your friend midsentence and start flirting with him.

B Raise your voice a bit so he hears what you're saying and jumps into your conversation.

C Huddle closer to your friend. You don't want him to think you're noticing him.

5 When your geometry teacher leaves the classroom after handing out a pop quiz, you:

A Use the time to scribble a flirty note and pass it to the cute guy two rows over.

B Exchange "bummer" looks with the guy you have a crush on, and then start on the first question.

C Take the quiz. Duh.

Mostly As: Certifiably guy-obsessed.

You probably already realize that guys take up a pretty big chunk of your brainpower. It's fun to be a little guy crazy, but when you're totally obsessed with them, you may be ignoring things you should be focusing on (like taking that quiz or enjoying that vacation!). Plus, when you slow down and figure out why you like each guy (cuteness factor aside), you'll have a better chance of connecting with one who's a great match for you. Which is way more fun than going after every guy you see just because you can.

Mostly Bs: Boys on the brain.

You've got the right idea about guys. You flirt with the ones you're crushing on, but flirting for flirting's sake doesn't do anything for you. Plus, your healthy attitude toward guys can actually help you get the guys you like: the fact that you've got interests outside of guys actually makes you more interesting to them. And bonus: when the right guy comes along, you won't need to date him—you'll want to!

Mostly Cs: Barely guy-conscious.

Guys take a backseat to all the other stuff you've got going on in your life, which is exactly how you want it. The way you see things, you're young, and there will be plenty of time for crushes and boyfriends later on, so there's no use obsessing now. And guess what? You're right. Keep on concentrating on doing the stuff you love, and when a guy who's intriguing enough comes along, you'll know it, and then you'll take notice. Just try not to roll your eyes too much at your boy-crazy friends, 'kay?

social life

Is she a true friend?

You *think* she means well, but you're not totally sure. Find out if she's got your best interests at heart.

1] **Last time you asked her if you looked okay, she:**

 A Looked you over, fixed a tag that was sticking out of your shirt, and then said you were good to go.

B Rolled her eyes and said, "You always look great!"

C Said, "You look hot!" but when you checked a mirror, you saw the giant piece of Twizzler in your teeth she neglected to tell you about.

2 When you both liked the same guy last year, she:

A Told you she'd rather give up the guy than risk ruining your friendship—and meant it.

B Said you should both forget about him but refused to discuss it any further.

C Told you he'd probably like you more but made a play for him behind your back anyway.

3 If you found out her family was moving to another state next year, you'd feel:

A Crushed. She's one of the only friends you truly trust.

B Bummed. She's really fun to hang out with, but you'll survive.

C Secretly relieved. Lately she's seemed like more of a competitor than a friend, anyway.

4 If you were going through something heavy with your boyfriend, you'd turn to her:

A First. She's never failed to listen and give you good advice.

B Maybe after you've already figured out what you wanted to do. She's a cool girl, but she never seems to really know what's best for you.

C Um, you probably wouldn't. You can't help feeling she has ulterior motives when she gives you advice.

5 Last time you told her a secret and asked her to please not tell anyone, she:

A Kept it to herself.

B Said okay, but somehow, another one of your friends found out about it.

C Promised she wouldn't, but the whole school was talking about it the next day.

[Mostly As] Friend till the end.

This girl's a keeper. She's a great listener and really seems to care about your happiness. When she gives you advice, you know she wants the best for you, because she's proved time and time again that she's for real. This girl values your friendship as much as you do, so let her know that you don't take it for granted. Be there for her through her ups and downs, just as she's there for you.

She wants the best for you.

[Mostly Bs] Fair-weather friend.

She's probably not a bad person, but it doesn't seem like she takes your friendship too seriously. Maybe it's just that she's more into partying than bonding, or maybe she's just a bit socially awkward. But she's not someone you can really confide in— or should. Keep being friends with her if you have fun together, but don't trust her with your innermost feelings. She may be a "fun" friend, but she's not showing you that she's best-friend material.

Don't trust her with your innermost feelings.

97

[Mostly Cs] Frienemy.

Sorry if this sounds harsh, but you've probably wondered the same thing: why are you even friends with this girl? Maybe she's just insecure about herself, but she seems intent on sabotaging you or embarrassing you in front of others. And she doesn't think twice about manipulating you to get what she wants. She's not a true friend to you, and her negative energy tends to get you down. It's doubtful that there's anything you can do to make her change her unfriendly ways, so phase her out of your life and focus on hanging out with people who actually care about you.

Phase her out of your life.

20

Are you a DOWNER?

Find out if you light up a room or if that raincloud following you around makes it all gloomy.

1) **Your best friend wants to try out for the cheerleading squad, but you know she doesn't have a chance of making it (um, her nickname is McKlutzy). So when she asks you what you think, you say:**

a) "Go for it, because even if you don't make it, you'll feel better for trying!"

b) "It seems like cheerleading is pretty hard to break into if you don't have a gymnastics background or you aren't friends with all the girls on the team. I think you'd be way better at cross-country."

c) "Don't do it. You won't make it anyway, so why risk making a fool of yourself?"

2) **Valentine's Day is coming up and you don't have a valentine this year. How will you mark the occasion?**

a) Make pink-frosted heart-shaped sugar cookies for everyone in your homeroom—and a few extras for your crush. Even if you don't have a special someone, why not spread the love?

b) Get together with your single girlfriends to watch videos and make dinner. You'll have so much fun, you won't even think about wanting a *date*-date.

c) Try to ignore the dumb carnation exchange and wall-to-wall red and pink at school as best you can. Why does no one ever talk about how evil and sadistic Cupid is?

3) **When your friend's boyfriend dumps her out of the blue and she needs a shoulder to cry on, how do you help?**

a) Give her a makeover and take her dancing. There are no blues a fun night out can't cure!

b) Tell her she's totally allowed to be devastated and angry, but there are tons of better guys who would fall all over themselves to date her when she's ready to move on.

c) Induct her into your Guys Are Scum society. Finally, she's seen the light about what jerks they all are.

4) You're running for class officer. What would most likely be your platform?

a) "You won't even recognize this school when I'm done improving it!"

b) "New vending machines that work, less homework per class, and a revamped school Web site that's easier to use. That's what you can expect if I'm elected."

c) "Things around here can't *get* any worse, but I'll do my best to get through to the administrators."

5) **You and your friends just saw the latest big romantic comedy. When you're all walking out of the theater, what are they saying to you?**

a) "OMG. *Every* movie we see becomes your new favorite movie!"

b) "Okay, that was pretty predictable, but we were totally cracking up during the part where . . ."

c) "Come on, it wasn't *that* bad! Stop making us feel guilty for wanting to see it!"

Mostly As
Nope, you're a princess of pep.

Your positivity meter is permanently cranked up to "through the roof." No matter how gloomy a situation, you always see the silver lining—and try to help others see it too. It's cool that you're so optimistic, but sometimes your cheerfulness can get overwhelming, especially to people who aren't as glass-half-full as you are (and admit it—most aren't). Not to say that you shouldn't be hopeful, but sugarcoating a bad situation—like when things aren't going well for a friend—just isn't helpful. Being realistic will help you just as much as your optimism, so instead of promising people the world, try promising them just what you're sure you can deliver.

Mostly Bs Nope, you're a realist.

You see things as they really are—when something great happens, you're psyched, and when something not-so-great goes down, you figure out how to deal with it and move on. It's awesome that you've realized that situations don't have to be all good or all crappy. Because of your level-headed attitude, your friends have come to count on you when they need an honest opinion, and you're happy to help.

Yep, you cast a shadow.

It's one thing to be realistic; it's another to be convinced that everything sucks, which seems to be your attitude. Yeah, life's not perfect, and lots of times it's far from it, but that doesn't mean you should just give up hope. Because good things do happen all the time. By only seeing the negative stuff, you're holding yourself back from enjoying the simple things (like vegging with friends or just relaxing at the movies), and worse, you're bringing everyone around you down too. You don't need to believe the world is all fairy dust and unicorns to have a little fun now and then. Just focus on the things that make you smile, and pretty soon, you'll notice that things suck a *little* less than you used to think.

fun life

What kind of STARLET would you be?

You'd have fame and fortune . . . now find out what you'd get in the tabloids for!

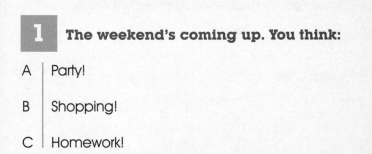

1 **The weekend's coming up. You think:**

A | Party!

B | Shopping!

C | Homework!

2 **People usually compliment you on:**

A | How much fun it is hanging out with you.

B | Your offbeat fashion sense.

C | Your ability to stay focused.

3 **You're drawn to guys who:**

A | Can keep up with your club-hopping on the weekends.

B | Are creative and arty.

C | Share your drive to do well in anything you attempt.

4 **You'd be happiest in a job that let you:**

A | Have a good time.

B | Express yourself.

C | Hone your craft.

5 **If you were going to the Oscars, you'd pick a dress that:**

A | Makes the most heads turn.

B | Is vintage and one of a kind.

C | Recalls a time of classic Hollywood glamour.

MOSTLY As: You'd be a socialite.

When people meet you, they think, "That girl's got charisma!" You don't wait for something fun to happen . . . the fun follows you. Like a socialite, you love going out, and admit only the most fabulous people to your inner circle. Enjoying life is your number one priority, but your carefree vibe may cause some people to take you less than seriously. Let people know you're fun and trustworthy by sticking to your promises and standing out in school, not just at parties.

Enjoying life is your number one priority.

MOSTLY Bs: You'd be a fashion icon.

You have a natural talent for putting together outfits people can't help wanting to look at—and then go home and copy! Whether you've combed the thrift stores for that perfect vintage top or ripped up some old clothes and made your own, you're a trendsetter

You're a trendsetter when it comes to expressing yourself.

when it comes to expressing yourself. Just like fashion icons people can't wait to see on the red carpet, you always steal the scene with your attention to detail and knack for making something ordinary unique. Just make sure you let others know you're about more than your style!

You want to be taken seriously for what you're doing.

Like a thespian, or serious actor, your craft is important to you. Whether you're working on a Brit lit paper or practicing for the school drama production, you won't stop fine-tuning your project until you're sure the result will be perfect. You don't really crave the spotlight as much as you want to be taken seriously for what you're doing— and your sophistication attracts people to you when they need solid advice. You really are a class act—just make sure to loosen up and enjoy the spotlight now and then!

22

Are you getting through to him?

Do you feel like he's always reading you wrong, or worse, just tuning you out? *How* you say stuff to guys is just as important as *what* you say.

1 **When you ask him if he likes your new jean skirt, he says, "Um, yeah, it's okay." What's your response?**

A "Oh my god, you totally think I look fat! Why would you say something so mean to me?"

B "Really? I think it's cute. Is there something you don't like about it?"

C "Oh." And vow to return it to the store tomorrow.

2 You're helping your guy study for his bio midterm. Even though you've been quizzing him with flash cards for hours, he's still not getting it. You find yourself:

A Snapping, "It's not that hard! DNA isn't the same as RNA . . . why can't you understand it?"

B Trying a new analogy that might help him understand it better.

C Repeating the difference between the two and silently hoping he catches on before it gets too late.

3 Your boyfriend of six months didn't call you last night like he said he would, and he didn't return your text, either. When you see him at school in the morning, you:

A March right up to him and say, "You said you'd call me and you didn't. What, do I not matter to you at *all* anymore?"

B "Hey, you, I was bummed we missed each other last night. Did you fall asleep early or something?"

C Wait for him to bring it up. If he doesn't, you just let it go.

4 If you wanted his advice about how to handle two of your best friends who aren't speaking, how would you ask?

A Explain every nuance of the situation (". . . and then Ashley wouldn't talk to Holly because she thought Holly said something behind Ashley's back but she actually didn't, but Ashley totally thought she did . . .") and ask him what he thinks.

B Say, "My friends are having a trust issue. Have any of your friends been through something like that? What do you think is the right thing to do?"

C Start asking him, then change your mind and say, "It's no big deal. Let's talk about something else."

5 You're hanging out with him and his friends and hear him mention that Natalie Portman was cute in her last movie. You say:

A "What?! That's an awful thing to say when your girlfriend is standing right here! Did you guys hear what he just said?"

B "But not as cute as me, right?" while giving him a wink.

C Nothing, but make a pouty face and shake your head at him in mock sadness.

Mostly As: No, you enter hostile territory.

It seems like when you try to be direct with him, your tone of voice can sound more upset than straightforward. When you seem upset and your guy doesn't think he did anything to cause it, he may get confused and tune out. To a guy, feeling blamed for something is a situation he probably associates more with an old babysitter than with a girlfriend! You probably don't like feeling as though he's always misreading you, so to avoid that in the future, try not to make it seem like a situation is more urgent than it is (maybe he was just distracted by something on TV and didn't even get a good look at your new skirt). Even if you're upset, stay calm, and never lash out at him in front of his friends, which can embarrass him and make you seem like the bad guy. After all, you want your guy to feel like you care about him, not like you're reprimanding him!

Mostly Bs: Yes, you're direct with him.

You've nailed the right way to communicate with your guy, which is pretty mature of you. You're patient with him, but you don't let him walk all over you either. You've realized that guys don't always respond the same way girls do—they tune out when you ramble on (even though you could ramble on to your best friend for hours and not lose her attention for a minute!). So if you need his advice, you relate your question to a situation he's been through. That way, he feels like he actually gets you, instead of being overwhelmed by "girl talk." You've also realized that if you need him to know something, you've got to tell him flat out (no beating around the bush). Right on!

Mostly Cs: Probably not.

After you learn this little secret, you might find that communicating with your guy just got much easier: guys don't get subtle hints. At all. It sounds like you have a hard time being straightforward about your feelings. But by being so indirect, you're preventing him from really getting to know you, and that'll make it difficult for you guys to grow closer. Next time you feel like everything you say disappears into a mysterious black hole in his mind, consider whether he just didn't get what you meant. If you want him to know something, you need to come right out and say it. Being clear doesn't mean being aggressive—you can still be the sweetie you are—but helping your guy out in the communication department will make things easier on both of you.

How **COMPETITIVE** are you?

They say life's a game. Find out if you're a bit too focused on that prize.

1] **When your history teacher is handing back your midterms, you are:**

A Craning your neck to see other people's grades. You better have gotten a higher grade than most of them!

B Exchanging "Please let us do well!" looks with the girl sitting next to you.

C Doodling in your notebook.

2] Both you and another girl are chatting up a cute guy you kind of know. When she tells a killer joke that cracks him up, you turn to her and say:

A "You know what else was funny? When you farted in math class yesterday!"

B "Oh my god, that was hilarious. It reminds me of this really funny story . . ."

C "I'm gonna go get some more soda now."

3] You're going to a party tonight with your best friend. When she calls to ask what you're wearing, you tell her:

A "Just what I wore to school today," but then change into your hottest dress. When you see her, you'll tell her you spilled something on your T-shirt.

B "My black boots, a skirt, and a green top." You don't want her to wear green too.

C "Just what I wore to school today." And actually mean it.

4] The way you see it, sites like MySpace are:

A Popularity contests, and with your hundreds of friends, you're pretty much winning!

B A fun way to talk to your friends and check out new music.

C Lame. Your life is nobody's business but yours.

5] A girl at school who has great style just got a new Marc by Marc Jacobs bag, which you love but totally can't afford. You:

A Blow your entire savings to get the slightly more expensive version. You can't stand that she has something so awesome and you don't.

B Treat yourself to a really cool knockoff and keep saving up for that car you want.

C Compliment her on it, saying you only wish you could be as fabulous as her.

[Mostly As] Bitter rival.

Whether you're dealing with grades, guys, or looks, you feel the need to always be ahead of everyone else. It's good to want to push yourself, but only when you're doing it for your own benefit. It seems you care more about how other people see you than how you see yourself, and you resort to some pretty mean (and catty!) measures to make sure you come out on top. Instead of focusing on what other people have that's better than what you have, focus on all the good stuff you've got going in your life. You'll realize it's a lot, and start feeling more secure. Plus, when others catch on that you're not always killing yourself to be the best, they'll see you as even more of a winner!

[Mostly Bs] Fair competitor.

You're an equal opportunity player. You know that sometimes you'll be the wittiest one in the room and sometimes you won't. But that doesn't stress you out or make you try to undermine others. You're secure with who you are, and realize that the beauty of people is that we're all different, and we all have amazing qualities. That chill outlook makes people feel totally at ease around you. Nice!

[Mostly Cs] Out of the game.

You don't feel comfortable competing with anyone for anything, so you take yourself completely out of the game. While it's cool to not want to fight for a guy or keep up with the big spenders, it's a shame that you're just standing on the sidelines, allowing everyone else to whiz past you. You deserve to feel that you're the top player sometimes too. So show that cute guy how funny you are, or make yourself feel good by putting on the outfit you feel your cutest in. It doesn't take much to get back in the running, and sometimes it feels good to play.

inner life

How **high maintenance** are you?

Find out if you're primp obsessed or upkeep optional.

1) When you were little, your go-to Halloween costume was:

a) A princess. You never wanted to look scary or ugly, so you went the pink dress/tiara route.

b) A witch. You got in the spirit with some green face paint.

c) A ghost. You'd just cut some holes in a sheet and you were off trick-or-treating. The candy is what you were after, so you didn't really care what you had to dress up as to get it.

2) After your shower, how long does it take you to get ready for school in the morning?

a) When you factor in makeup, hair, and several outfit changes, it comes to around two hours.

b) About a half hour to get dressed and ready and an extra ten minutes to down some cereal.

c) Shower?

3) You just blew out your hair before going out with friends, and the second you step outside it starts to pour. You're already running late, so you:

a) Text your friends that you can't make it. If you're going to look like a frizzball, what's the point of going out at all?

b) Run inside to grab an umbrella and your rubber rain boots, if you can find them.

c) Dash to your car. What can you do—your hair's doomed anyway.

4) If you could get a new puppy tomorrow, what kind would you get?

a) A bichon frise. They look like little white powder puffs, and one would totally fit in your cute new logo bag.

b) A pug. They're so cute (in an ugly sort of way) and funny, even if they are loud breathers.

c) A golden retriever. They're always up for whatever, and love playing Frisbee in the mud.

5) Your favorite shoes are:

a) Sky-high strappy sandals that you paid half your savings for. And they're worth it!

b) Your Chuck Taylors. They go with everything and add instant cool.

c) If you can't go barefoot? Your ratty flip-flops from two years ago.

Haute couture.

You don't feel ready unless you've plucked, primped, and prettied yourself, even if it takes you hours! You pay attention to labels and looks, and you'll be the first to admit that appearances mean a lot to you. It's cool to want to be your best, but when your focus on looking good prevents you from living your life, then we have a problem. Sure, you want your hair to be perfect, but try to take it easy on the primping and the need for status clothes. Your true friends will still love you if you have a bit of bedhead—in fact, they'll probably be relieved that they don't have to wait for you to painstakingly perfect your hair. Again! And to tell the truth, being imperfect is a lot more fun!

Mostly Bs Off the rack.

You like to look cute as much as the next girl, but you don't put everything on the back burner just because of a little humidity. People love being around you because you know when to dress up and when to live it up (sometimes at the same time!). In your mind, having a good laugh with friends is more important than having the new "it" bag. And that's just how it should be!

Mostly Cs Workout gear.

No one's ever accused you of being a diva! You don't put much importance on how you look—you're pretty much the roll-out-of-bed-and-go type. It's awesome that you're so unsuperficial, but how you present yourself on the outside gives others a clue to how you feel on the inside. So when you're always wearing the same grimy T-shirt, people may start thinking you just don't care about how they see you, or worse, that you don't value yourself! You don't have to wear a dress and curl your hair, but try to mix up your look a bit to seem more put-together, especially when there's a special occasion like an internship interview or assembly. You might just find that you get taken a lot more seriously!

25

What **BIG CITY** should you live in?

Find out which bustling metropolis would make you feel at home.

 1   **If your friends had to pick one word to describe you, they'd probably go with:**

A | Intense.

B | Outgoing.

C | Warm.

2   **Which of these shoes would you buy first?**

A | Knee-high black leather boots.

B | Strappy metallic heels.

C | Cute flats.

3 **If you could shadow any businesswoman for a day, you'd choose:**

A   A fashion designer or magazine editor.

B   A movie producer or an actress.

C   The CEO of a nonprofit company or a college professor.

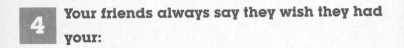 **4** **Your friends always say they wish they had your:**

A   Creativity and drive.

B   Social skills and sense of adventure.

C   Gentle spirit and politeness.

 **5** **You're in your element when you're:**

A   Having a deep philosophical discussion.

B   Dancing at a big, rocking party.

C   Helping a friend with her problems.

MOSTLY As: New York City.

You thrive under pressure, so the bustling pace of NYC would be a perfect match for your intense energy. Creative and full of ideas, you'd feel right at home in a big, diverse

effortless cool

city like New York, where people from all over the world come together to trade innovative thoughts and make it to the top of their field, whether it's the arts, publishing, or business. And bonus: your effortless cool will make you seem like a born New Yorker. See you on the subway!

MOSTLY Bs: Los Angeles.

You'd fit right in with the glitz and glamour of L.A. A town centered on entertainment (um, and awesome weather!), Los Angeles is the ideal home for someone with a big personality and a love of big events, like you. You always

glitz and glamour

know about the next big thing right before it breaks, and people look to you to set trends and start the party. All those qualities will make you feel right at home in Hollywood!

127

You prefer a more laid-back lifestyle to a work- or party-driven one, so Chicago is the city for you. It's big enough for you to accomplish all your goals in life but seems homey and warm, so you never feel anonymous—maybe that's why Oprah films her show there. You're close with your family, and your friends know to come to you when they need advice—and that you're more than willing to stop what you're doing and help them. You're a Midwestern girl at heart, so Chicago is your home, sweet home.

homey and warm

26

Are you **toying** with your guy?

Find out if you play by the rules in the game of love.

1 When your friend breaks up with her boyfriend because he cheated on her, the first thing you do is:

A Call your guy and tell him how glad you are that you're honest with each other.

B Double-check all the comments on your boyfriend's MySpace page to search for hidden innuendos from his female friends.

C Create a fake MySpace profile with a picture of a really cute girl who shares all your boyfriend's interests, then try to "friend" him and see what he does.

2 Your guy's out with his boys, and you're at a party with your girlfriends. When a hot guy you've never met starts flirting with you and asks you for your number so he can text you, you:

A Tell him you're flattered but you can't give it out because you're with someone.

B Keep flirting with him all night but stop short of giving him your number. If he's really interested, he can find you online.

C Say sure, and program it into his phone. He doesn't even go to your school, so your boyfriend will never find out about your new text buddy.

3 You can't stand one of your guy's friends, Jake, who you think is an awful influence on him. So you:

A Make other plans whenever your guy's hanging out with Jake.

B Start calling his friend "Jake the Jerk." Maybe your guy will catch on.

130

C Start a cruel rumor that Jake is only friends with your guy as a joke (and make sure it gets back to your boyfriend). Maybe that'll get him to stop being friends with that loser for good.

4 You and your ex are friends again, and he asks you on Monday to hang out that Friday (date night!). You say:

A "Sorry, I've got plans that night, but what about Wednesday?"

B "Maybe—let me think about it." That way, if your current guy's not up for hanging out that night, you've got a backup!

C "Sure." Your bf hasn't said anything about hanging out on Friday yet, so you have to teach him a lesson that he has to act faster if he wants time with you.

5 When you're mad at your guy, you:

A Explain to him what made you so upset. He usually apologizes and then you guys make up.

B List all the things he did wrong that he needs to apologize to you for.

C Bring up every mean, rude, or clueless thing he's ever done or said to you, even if it was a year ago and you've never brought it up before.

Mostly As: Playing fair.

As far as love goes, you're a great sport. You treat your guy with the honesty and respect you expect him to give you in return. Just make sure that in your quest for fairness, you don't hold back from telling him what you need from the relationship, like if you want to nail down your plans earlier in the week. As long as you're equal players, he'll be glad to help you win together.

Mostly Bs: Fun and games.

A lot of the time, you're pretty up-front with your guy. But in certain situations, like when you're feeling mad or insecure or when another guy shows interest, you don't always play so fair. It's cool to want to look out for your own interests, and you're young, so you probably feel like you and your bf won't be together forever anyway. But take a look at your relationship and ask yourself if you're really happy in it. If you think it's worth working for, then be more direct with your guy instead of dropping hints or using sneaky tactics.

Mostly Cs: Toy story.

Not to be harsh, but it sounds like you're more into manipulating your guy than dating him. Maybe you've been hurt by guys in the past, or you're just not into this one, but try to realize that he's not always the bad guy and you're not always the good guy. Think about how you'd feel if he was always sneaking around behind your back doing things you probably wouldn't approve of. You'd be upset, right? He doesn't want to be toyed with either. So if you want to make this relationship work, you need to stop lying to him now (and anyway, it's not a good habit to bring to your future relationships). Good relationships are based on trust and respect. If you're not ready to change your ways, then maybe you're just not into being part of a couple right now.

What's your **friendship** role?

Find out what job you'd hold if your social life were the professional world!

1] **When a friend tells you she got food poisoning, your first thought is to:**

A Start planning a "Glad you're feeling better" night out for when she's back to normal.

B Remind her to drink plenty of fluids and eat bland foods until she starts feeling better.

C Bring her some homemade soup and take notes for her during the days she misses school.

2] A girl you know from another school invites you to a party she's having next weekend. You immediately ask her:

A If you can bring all your friends.

B What her friends are like. Before you ask anyone to come with you, you want to make sure they'd have a good time.

C If you can bring any food or help her set up.

3] Your friend likes a guy who clearly doesn't know she's alive. To help her out, you:

A Figure out where he'll be next weekend and show up with her so he has a chance to get to know her in a fun atmosphere.

B Ask her what she thinks they have in common and tell her to bring that subject up next time she's around him.

C Gush about how awesome she is next time you see him in art class.

4 You get three IMs from three different people within the span of a minute. Two out of three are:

A Friends asking what's up for this weekend.

B Friends asking for your famous guy advice.

C Friends asking if you can give them a ride somewhere.

5 A new girl starts at your school and seems pretty cool. You think she's friend material, so you:

A Arrange a fun bowling night so all your other friends can meet her.

B Chat her up in the lunchroom to find out her interests.

C Ask her if she needs someone to show her around the neighborhood.

[Mostly As] Party planner.

You're the go-to girl in your group of friends when it comes to figuring out what to do next weekend. Your buds know that with you around, there's no chance they'll be sitting home alone. You always know about the hottest parties, and you're never afraid to get your friends to branch out and try new things (or meet new guys!). Plus,

There's always new fun to be had.

you're always reading up on movies and concerts, so there's always new fun to be had. If you want to change it up, let someone else do the planning sometimes. You just might find that it's fun to go along for the ride once in a while!

[Mostly Bs] Guidance counselor.

If your social life were a road trip, you'd be the one holding the map. Your friends trust your judgment, and your advice has always led them in the right direction. They value your honesty and tact when it comes to the important

Your advice-giving skills are awesome.

things, like their dating lives. With you around, they know they'll always have someone to set them back on track if they veer off. But even though your advice-giving skills are awesome, remember to let your friends find their own way sometimes too.

[Mostly Cs] Caregiver.

You're always there, ready to help.

Your friends appreciate your willingness to come to their aid. Whether they're sick and need chicken soup or they need help studying for a test, you're always there, ready to help. That nurturing nature of yours makes people feel calm and cared for in your presence. But make sure your friends offer you the same support you're always giving them.

Are you in a **rut**?

Spinning your wheels and getting nowhere?
Consider this quiz your gateway to a fresh start.

1) **You've been semistalking the same elusive boy for six months. You know how he likes his eggs (with hot sauce) and what shampoo he uses, but you have yet to flirt with him. What do you do now?**

a) Put the word out that you may be interested and see what happens.

b) Probably just more detective work from afar. You've gotten pretty good at it—thanks, *CSI*!

c) Convince yourself that if nothing's happened yet, it never will. Time to move on to the next crush.

2) Fashion-wise, you're the type who:

a) Follows every trend like your life depends on it. What's the fun of having only one style?

b) Picks up a few pieces that are "in" each season, but only the ones you know will look good on you.

c) Still wears the same types of T-shirts and jeans you did as a kid. It's worked for you this long, and the thought of changing things up now is kind of daunting.

3) You've been a writer ever since you can remember. What's the current state of your work?

a) You submit a few stories or poems a year to your school's literary magazine—the ones you're really proud of.

b) You've got dozens of half-finished drafts under your bed and are currently writing three more.

c) Uh, what work? You haven't written a word in six months, and now you're starting to feel like you have nothing to say.

4) **If you asked your parents whether your best friend, Jenny, can come over for dinner, they'd most likely say:**

a) "Which friend again? It seems like you get a new best friend every month!"

b) "Sure. You and Jenny have gotten so close this year, haven't you?"

c) "Okay, but don't you want to invite someone new to dinner once in a while? We love Jenny, but we see her all the time."

5) **It's a new school year and you have to start signing up for school clubs and sports. What's your game plan?**

a) Try out for hockey (you did track last year), join the school paper (you did yearbook last year), and sign on to art club (you did environmental club last year).

b) Stay on the teams you're good at, but replace a club you didn't really dig last year with a new one. Plus, this year, you're planning on finding an after-school job.

c) Do the same stuff as last year. Why mess with what you know?

Mostly As Lead foot.

It's one thing to have a lot of different interests—it's another to have a different interest every week! While it's great that you don't seem to get into those run-of-the-mill ruts that bring people down, constantly jumping from one new passion to the next is its own kind of rut, when you really think about it. If you quit field hockey after a bad game or write off a guy after hanging out once, you could be limiting yourself by not giving your current interest a chance to play out—kind of like listening to the first half of a song and stopping it without ever getting to the best part. So give yourself a chance to get used to new friends or clubs. You just might find some things worth sticking with.

Mostly Bs Full speed ahead.

When it comes to mixing it up, you are a certified master. You know when to change your situation if it's not working out (like that doomed-from-the-start summer fling), but you also stick with things long enough to give them a chance (Who'd have thought you'd become such a whiz at Photoshop?). You're always willing to try new things, so you never find yourself bored with your life.

Mostly Cs Flat tire.

Welcome to Rutsville. Population: more people than you think. Everyone gets into ruts. Whether your relationship is getting stale or a certain fight with your parents brings on major déjà vu, it's normal to feel like you've hit a speed bump once in a while. But if it seems like your whole life is in a general funk and you have no interest in trying new things (or worse, you've lost interest in things you used to love), that could signify a more serious problem, such as depression or social anxiety. Take heart—there's hope for escaping almost any rut. The first step is to figure out what rut you're in (family rut, friend rut, creative rut, etc.), then decide to take baby steps out of it. So join one new group or buy one cute (and different) pair of shoes. You'll find yourself on cruise control in no time.

29

How **gullible** are you?

Could you be too wide-eyed for your own good? Take this quiz to find out.

1) **A cute guy you meet at a concert concession stand asks for your number. You walk away thinking:**

a) "Oh my god, that was just like a scene from a romantic comedy. What if he's the one?"

b) "He was hot. Wonder if he'll actually call?"

c) "He seemed way out of my league. There must be something wrong with him."

2) **When you started going to sleepovers, it seemed like your friends were always:**

a) Freezing your bra, drawing on your forehead while you were sleeping, and playing any other practical jokes they could think of on you! It totally wasn't fair!

b) Eating junk food, spilling secrets, and giving each other makeovers.

c) Trying to convince you that the Ouija board was scary, not funny.

3) You hear that one of your friends is spreading rumors about you. What's the first thing you do?

a) Tell whoever told you that it isn't possible. None of your friends would ever say anything bad about you.

b) Try to figure out why she could possibly be mad at you and keep your ears open to see if you hear anything else, but hold off on confronting her just yet.

c) March right up to her, tell her you can't believe she betrayed you, and call her some unflattering names. You can't let her get away with this.

4) A man approaches your group of friends at a mall and tells you he thinks you guys would make great extras on a film he's directing in your city. Your response?

a) "Really? I'm so flattered. When's the shoot?"

b) "Um, I'm not sure. Give me your card and I'll think about it."

c) "Get away from us, you creep."

5) When you're up late at night and an infomercial comes on about some product that claims to do it all, you tend to:

a) Watch the whole thing. You're obsessed with infomercials and have even ordered stuff from them before.

b) Watch for a bit, then flip to something else. It all seems too good to be true.

c) Watch it while making fun of those sad people promoting their sad products. Who in their right mind believes a blender can clean itself?

Mostly As Easy target.

You've always been trusting of everyone, which is cool because it means you see the best in people. But taking everything at face value can backfire, whether it's just friends playing little pranks on you because they can, or something a bit more serious, like meeting someone online whose motivation isn't only friendship. You don't have to stop trusting people, just try being a little more skeptical of situations that seem too good to be true. When you learn to follow your gut, it usually leads you in the right direction!

Mostly Bs Savvy skeptic.

You give people the benefit of the doubt, but you've got a great sense of when something doesn't seem quite right. You've found a great balance between being just cynical enough and knowing how to let your guard down and have a great time. People know they don't have to go out of their way to convince you of something they're saying (like a friend who insists she really didn't talk behind your back), but they know they can't pull one over on you either!

Mostly Cs Seriously cynical.

You've got your defenses up all the time. Everything is suspicious to you until proven otherwise, and you're always looking for signs that a situation isn't what it looks like. It's smart not to believe everything you see and hear, but it's exhausting when you're always second-guessing everyone around you, including your friends! If you make them back up everything they're saying, they'll start resenting that you don't trust them—not good. Try letting your guard down more and accepting some things as they are. It's more fun to just enjoy life than to constantly scrutinize it.

fun life

Are you too PLUGGED IN?

Find out if all that digital juggling is scrambling your brain.

 When your favorite show is on, you're usually:

A | Watching it while IMing your friends and surfing the Internet.

B | Paying attention to it, but you text your friends when something crazy happens.

C | Glued to the screen, and that's it.

 The holiday season's here. How do you buy gifts for your friends and fam?

A | Totally online.

B | You flip through magazines and catalogs, then either buy stuff online or hit the stores to get it.

C | You go to the mall. Duh.

3 **Your friend just broke up with her boyfriend yesterday. How did you find out?**

A | On her friends-only LiveJournal post or MySpace page.

B | She texted you after it happened.

C | She told you in person at school today.

4 **How many gadgets (like your cell phone, iPod, camera, etc.) do you have to charge regularly?**

A | More than five.

B | Two to four.

C | Just one.

5 **You don't know how people ever lived without:**

A | The Internet, cell phones, iPods, BlackBerries, video games, blogs, MySpace, Mp3s—the list goes on.

B | The Internet, cell phones, and iPods.

C | The Internet.

MOSTLY As: Blowing a fuse.

Your room looks like an electronics store exploded in there! You're into the latest, hottest gadgets, and you feel naked without at least a handful of things that beep, buzz, or light up. It's one thing to be great at multitasking (which you totally are), but it's another to live life via texts, blogs, and MySpace. By connecting with people mostly through technology, you're missing out on the real-life interactions that sharpen your social skills—which are even more crucial

You feel naked without at least a handful of things that beep, buzz, or light up.

than tech skills to being a success later in life. Try to cut down on your tech use, 'cause you can't just log out of real-world situations!

MOSTLY Bs: Plugged in.

You've found a way to make technology work for you without letting it take over your life. Sure, you love your iPod and your cell, but you're not rushing out to get every new model of every new gadget. You know when to IM or text a friend, but you'd never do that when there was something important going on with her.

> You've found a way to make technology work for you.

You've wisely discovered that some things need to be dealt with face to face, not Send button to Send button. Smarty.

MOSTLY Cs: Tuned out.

You couldn't care less about technology. Frankly, the fact that everyone's so obsessed with the newest, smallest, and most advanced phones and gadgets kind of bugs you—you wish things could just be simple, the way they were in the nondigital past. It's great that you know how to lead a full life without your bag beeping or buzzing every five minutes, but totally ignoring all innovations isn't good either, since you'll need to keep up to stay competitive in your future work life. You don't need to become a tech head, just try not to shun everything new and improved.

You'll need to keep up to stay competitive.

love life

What kind of **FLIRT** are you?

Find out what your guy-getting style says
about you.

1 **You hit it off with a sweet, cute guy at your
cousin's party, exchange e-mails, and
agree to look each other up on MySpace. The
next day, you:**

A Send him a sweet, flattering e-mail about
how funny he was last night.

B Include him on a group e-mail telling
people to go check out a friend's band next
weekend.

C Don't write him, but ask your best guy
friends to post flirty messages on your MySpace
so your crush sees how in demand you are.

2 You spot your crush two checkout lines away at the drugstore—just as he's about to turn your way and see you. Your flirting strategy?

A Be looking straight at him when he turns toward you, and give him a smile and a wink.

B Wait for him to say hey, then say, "Quit stalking me! It's getting creepy."

C Pretend you don't see him, but when you're sure he's looking, act sexy: flip your hair, touch your neck, and pretend you're deep in thought.

3 What's the most out-there thing you've ever done to get a crush's attention?

A Walked right up to him, tapped him on the shoulder, and said, "Hey, foxy. Wanna make out?"

B Spread the word through mutual friends that you might be into him.

C Found out what his favorite band was, then, when you knew he'd be passing by, raved to your best friend about how much you love them.

4 Your friend is *in looove* with a guy in your art class who she swears doesn't know she exists. Your advice to her is:

A "Come by after our class and all-out flirt with him. Being bold about it is the only way he'll really notice you."

B "Okay, I'll ask this girl Kat in our class to mention your name when we're all standing around. Then I'll tell you what he says."

C "For our art exhibit, he's doing a painting of a girl in a gray dress. We'll go shopping and get you a dress just like it to wear. When he sees you, he'll definitely notice!"

5 OMG! He finally texts you and asks if you want to hang out next weekend! What do you text back?

A "Hello, I thought you'd never ask!"

B "Um, why would I want to hang out with you? (J/K!)"

C "Interesting proposition. Let me think about it and get back to you."

Mostly As: Focused.

You've got no problem letting a guy know you're into him, as your fearless flirting style reveals. When you want someone, you put on your flirtiest smile and let the compliments fly. And you're the kind of girl who's not scared of rejection. Your theory is, if he's not into you, it's his loss! It's great to be confident, but make sure you know a bit about the guy you've got your sights set on before your flirting goes from zero to sixty. Some guys like the direct effect, but others are put off by over-the-top displays of infatuation. Your love life will benefit when you realize there are times to crank up the flirt factor and times to tone it down a bit.

Your theory is, if he's not into you, it's his loss!

Mostly Bs: Roundabout.

If you're not a hundred percent sure he's into you too, you're not one to risk rejection with a superdirect flirting style. Instead, you go the indirect route, planting hints through friends and using sarcasm as a way to keep your true feelings semihidden. It's totally normal—and understandable!—to want to feel the situation out before letting on that you like him. But by being so indirect, you risk making him confused. If you invite him and all his friends to a show or hit him with mock insults, he might never even sense that you like him at all, which definitely won't help your case. Try sending him some clearer signals, like after you send that group e-mail, send only him a text that says "You better go!" That way, you'll be giving away just enough to get him interested.

> By being so indirect, you risk making him confused.

Mostly Cs: Stealthy.

You're so great at being subtle that you might want to consider a career in the CIA! Problem is, guys aren't so great at picking up on subtle signals. (That's why you've probably noticed that your crushes never seem to catch on that you like them! Frustrating, right?) You're on the right track by finding out about his interests and making sure you've got stuff in common. That'll give you something to talk about when you finally, you know, talk!

You've got to be bolder about letting him know you like him.

But to get to that point, you've got to be bolder about letting him know you like him. Next time he's wearing a cool T-shirt, compliment him on it instead of rushing out to find it in your size and wearing it the next day. Or if you find him looking your way in class, give him a slightly longer-than-normal smile back. You might think you're being way obvious, but it could be just enough to start something great with him.

32

Do you live for **gossip**?

We all love a juicy story now and then, but find out if you thrive on hearing—and spreading around—other people's business.

1 You overhear the head cheerleader (and school snob) bawling in the bathroom and telling her friend, "It's over!" So you:

A Run out and text a bunch of people that Barbie and Ken are kaput.

B Figure she's got some relationship troubles and see if anyone says anything about it later.

C Pee and then go to class. Whatever's wrong is none of your business.

2 Your friend's going out with her longtime crush for the first time tonight. When she gets home and calls you, you:

A Demand to know every single detail, starting from the beginning. She better not leave anything out!

B Ask her how it went.

C Can't wait to talk about the latest episode of the TV show she missed while she was out.

3 When you hear that your ex hooked up with someone in your grade, you:

A Ask every one of your mutual friends who it was. You can't bear not knowing who replaced you!

B Are curious but don't go out of your way to find out who it was. You don't want to seem obvious.

C Roll your eyes and wonder why people still think you care.

4] After your history class, you find a note someone dropped on the ground that says "JS and RR are totally hooking up, but don't tell anyone!" That night, you:

A Put off your homework to search your yearbook for who JS and RR could be.

B Mention it to your friend when she calls but figure it could be anyone.

C Go to practice, have dinner, do your homework, etc. You forgot about that note the second after you read it.

5] At a party, you can usually be found:

A Observing people and who they're talking to, then whispering to your friends about the latest potential couples.

B Having fun with your friends and maybe meeting some cool new people.

C Only talking to people you know. To be honest, you don't really like parties anyway.

[Mostly As] Gossipmonger.

When it comes to gossip, you can't seem to get enough! You get a huge rush from finding out who hooked up with who, or why some couple broke up, and you relish being the first to know something. It's normal to want to be clued in to what's going on around you, but it seems like you place more importance on finding out what's up in other people's lives than you do on living your own life, which isn't so cool. For starters, if friends know you're always blabbing, they'll stop trusting you. And people won't take you seriously if gossip is all you're about. Try focusing more on yourself and less on what everyone else is doing. You just might find that by filling your life with stuff that makes you happy, you won't need to live vicariously through others.

[Mostly Bs] Informed, not obsessed.

You've got a healthy appetite for buzz, but it doesn't keep you from living your life. Sure, you're interested when you hear that the "it" couple broke up, but you don't feel the need to show people how clued in you are by texting everyone you know. When friends come to you for advice, they know you can be trusted. You're secure in your own life, and that makes people want to be around you—which should make you feel great.

[Mostly Cs] In the dark.

You couldn't care less who broke up with who last weekend, and that's totally cool. Your life is full enough without cluttering things up with useless information about people you don't even care about. Gossip seems so frivolous to you, and lots of times it is. But when it comes to your friends, make sure you show them that even though you don't really care about what's-her-face in bio, you care a whole lot about what happens in their lives. Knowing what's up with your friends will not only strengthen your bond with them, but it'll make you feel a little more up-to-date.

33

What kind of **DREAMER** are you?

What you think about when your head's in the clouds says a lot about you.

1) **You're bored and staring out the window in study hall. Where does your mind wander?**

a) To how you'll be running your own business one day.

b) To your perfect wedding day, with all your loved ones there.

c) To a random thought, like what it would be like to make a sandwich in space or play in an underwater playground.

2) Your ideal guy would have to be:

a) As smart and driven as you are.

b) Superexpressive about his feelings, and romantic.

c) Out of the ordinary.

3) Your favorite part of the day is:

a) Sunrise—you love feeling like you could accomplish anything.

b) Dusk—it's so beautiful and comforting.

c) Two a.m.—anything can happen when it's pitch-black outside!

4) You tend to get frustrated if you:

a) Aren't the best at what you're doing.

b) Can't make things work in a relationship or friendship.

c) Feel constrained by other people's rules.

5) **You wouldn't be *you* without:**

a) Your goals.

b) Your ideals.

c) Your imagination.

Mostly As Ambitious.

You aren't afraid to dream big. When your mind wanders, it goes to your future, where you

> You envision accomplishing great things.

envision accomplishing great things and growing into a strong, powerful woman. Those aren't just vague dreams, though. You're practical enough to split your big ideas into smaller goals and set out to reach them one by one. Your dreams are sophisticated, but don't stop yourself from letting your mind wander to crazy places you don't normally let yourself go. With your beyond-your-years maturity and a bit of imagination, there won't be any big dreams you can't accomplish.

Mostly Bs Romantic.

You're a true idealist. Your mind conjures up images of fairy-tale romances and a world where everyone is happy . . . and in your heart, you see no reason why you won't fall in love with Mr. Right or see world peace in your lifetime. You're supersensitive to the needs of those around you, and people feel comforted in your presence. Some might tell

> You conjure up images of a world where everyone is happy.

you to keep dreaming, because your lofty goals will never come true. But ignore them. As long as you approach your ideals with a bit of practicality, there's no reason you should give them up.

Original.

Some people think you're quirky or offbeat, and you know what? They're right. But you're wacky in a good way—like a creative genius way! You were the kid who always colored outside the lines and made up your own bedtime stories. And now your mind is bursting with tons of innovative thoughts and out-there ideas. When you're talking, you tend to go off on tangents, and rules and regulations make you crazy. Try channeling that offbeat brilliance by writing down all your crazy thoughts. Who knows . . . you could stumble onto a new invention that might make you millions.

Your mind is bursting with tons of innovative thoughts.

34

Is your friend
HOLDING YOU BACK?

Sure, you've been buds with her since
kindergarten, but that doesn't mean she's
still best-friend material.

1] **You're trying to decide what to do for your
birthday this year. She'd most likely suggest:**

A Sneaking into an over-eighteen club, even
though you're not eighteen yet. Her present to
you would be a fake ID.

B Renting movies and pigging out on junk food—
just the two of you.

C Getting a bunch of friends together for dinner
at your favorite restaurant.

2 You're out bathing-suit shopping for the Caribbean vacation you're going on with your family. When you're in the dressing room, she's:

A Too busy trying on skimpy bikinis to give you much feedback.

B Telling you the two suits you already have at home are fine.

C Waiting for you so she can tell you what she thinks.

3 You guys are supposed to see a movie at two o'clock. It's one-fifty and you're in the snack line. Where's your friend?

A Flirting with the guys who work at the arcade next door. She's always late for some reason or another.

B Telling you that she read horrible reviews of the movie you're about to see.

C Next to you, deciding whether to get Goobers or Sour Patch Kids.

4] What does your mom think of her?

A She's a bit self-centered and a bad influence.

B She's exactly the same as she was in the third grade.

C She's a smart girl and a good friend to you.

5] When you tell her you have a crush on someone, she almost always:

A Starts flirting with him too.

B Bad-mouths him in hopes that you won't get a boyfriend.

C Helps you figure out ways you can see him outside of school.

[Mostly As]
Yep, she's a drama magnet.

You know how you always get this nagging feeling that she's not as invested in your friendship as you are? You're probably on to something. Not to say that she was never a good friend to you, because maybe at one point she was. But right now, she's more focused on herself, and wants everyone else to be too. She may just be going through a phase where she wants to be the wild child or the center of attention, but when she hangs out with you, she almost always views the night as another episode of *The [Her Name Here] Show*. As far as she's concerned, she's the star and you're the sidekick, and as long as you let her steal your spotlight, you won't get your chance to shine. Start seeing less of her and more of the friends who value you enough to let you be the star you truly are.

[Mostly Bs]
Yep, she's kind of a dud.

Sounds like you've moved on from the days of teddy bears and sleepovers. Her? Not so much. Your friend is probably nostalgic for those simple days when it was just the two of you, with no complications like boys or parties. But the truth is, you've outgrown her and the tastes you used to share (which is why it probably seems like she shoots down every movie you want to see). It can be frustrating when you and a formerly close friend seem to be on completely different wavelengths, but she just needs time to catch up to you or grow into her own, more mature self. Don't cut ties with her, but don't let her hold you back from the stuff you like doing, either.

[Mostly Cs] Nope, she's still your partner in crime.

You guys are still two peas in a pod. Growing up has actually made your bond stronger instead of making you drift apart. You're pretty lucky to have a friend who's been with you for so long and still gets you and wants the best for you. In fact, you've been by her side so long that she sometimes feels like your twin, so make sure you guys give each other enough space to develop your own tastes and interests apart from one another. That way you'll have even more to share when you're together.

fun life

How do you PARTY?

Stuck by the wall or in the middle of the action?
Identify your party persona.

 Your teacher is called out of class to take a phone call, so you:

A | Get up in front of the class and start pretend-teaching and cracking jokes.

B | Step in and make sure things don't get too out of hand while you guys have no supervision.

C | Quietly sit there and check out what everyone does while the teach is away.

 Your friends are planning a trip to an amusement park. When you all get there, you:

A | Convince your friends to head straight to the biggest, scariest roller coaster.

B | Whip out the park map and devise a game plan for the group.

C | Can't help feeling overwhelmed at all the crazy rides and hordes of people.

3 **You hear your crush likes you back (yes!). Your next step is to:**

A | Walk up to him and strike up a conversation.

B | Get a mutual friend to nonchalantly ask him if it's true.

C | Check out if he acts any different toward you and wait for him to make his move.

4 **It's Friday night, and you and your friends are planning on going to the movies. Your job is:**

A | Picking the movie.

B | Getting everyone up to speed on your meeting time and place.

C | Sparking a discussion about the movie after you see it.

 5 **If you had to join one, you'd most likely sign up for:**

A | Pep squad.

B | Prom planning committee.

C | School newspaper.

MOSTLY As: The life of the party.

You love getting out there in the middle of things, and at a party, you can be found tearing up the dance floor with your moves or cracking up the crowd with your hilarious stories. You're bold and full of life, and people love partying with you because they find your endless energy infectious!

MOSTLY Bs: The heart of the party.

If you're not the host of the party, then you probably helped plan it or got people to come. Either way, you thrive when you're putting your amazing organizational skills to good use . . . like making sure people have enough snacks and drinks and everyone is having a good time. When you're around, people know they'll be taken care of.

MOSTLY Cs: The party's people-watcher.

You like to stand back and take things in, and at parties, you find nothing more fun than watching everyone do their thing. That's not to say that you don't like having a good time, too—you totally do. But instead of being in the middle of things, you like to hang out on the outskirts and be a bit mysterious. When people want to know how a party went or who hooked up with who, they come right to you for all the answers, O observant one!

What **role** does he play in your life?

If your life were a movie, find out if your guy would be up for an Oscar.

1 **You're really hoping to get a spot on your school's softball team. In the weeks leading up to tryouts, your guy:**

A Plans out a detailed practice regimen for you, including intense drills for a few hours each day—under his supervision, of course.

B Comes by to throw a ball around with you a few times a week to help you get better at pitching.

C Doesn't even realize you're planning on trying out.

2 You've got girls' night and he's got guys' night. While you're out, he:

A Calls you every hour to give you a play-by-play of the funny things his friends just did or said.

B Texts you once during the night to tell you he can't wait to hang out tomorrow.

C Does his own thing without getting in touch.

3 When it comes to your group of friends, he:

A Has made a point of meeting every single friend, memorizing her vital stats, and forming solid opinions about whether she's a good or bad friend to you.

B Knows and gets along with most of them.

C Hasn't met the majority, and never really shows an interest in meeting them.

4 When you call him all upset about a fight you had with your parents, your boyfriend:

A Insists on coming over and mediating a discussion between you and your mom and dad.

B Stays on the phone with you for as long as you need, and offers his advice when you ask for it.

C Says, "Bummer," and then tells you he's in the middle of something and will call you back.

5 The two of you are hanging out at a party with a bunch of kids from another school who you don't know. How does he act?

A He keeps one arm around you all night, while using the other to act out the loud jokes he's telling.

B He's cool with both of you mingling and meeting new people but regularly winks at you across the room or asks if you need another soda.

C You can't really tell, since you don't know where he went for a big chunk of the night.

Mostly As: He steals the spotlight.

If your guy has your best interests at heart, then he has a
pretty weird way of showing it. From the way he insists on
making sure he plays the lead role in your life, you'd
think he wanted to be your director, not your boyfriend.
And no matter what the situation, he's intent on being
the one in the spotlight. If things go on this way, you'll
miss out on your chance to shine, so let him know that
it's not cool for him to feel like he has a say in everything
you do—or for him to overshadow you. Next time you're
out with friends, tell him girls-only means no phone calls
either. And when he starts to plan something out for you,
let him know you can handle it on your own. If he still
acts controlling, then maybe you should rethink whether
you're happy in this relationship. It's no fun letting
someone else be the star in the movie of your life!

Mostly Bs: He's your leading man.

This one's got Oscar potential. He's strong and sensitive,
and most importantly, he doesn't stifle your star
potential. In fact, he encourages you to do your best at
everything you try. When you need help, he's there for

you, but he doesn't insist on butting in when you're already in control. Whatever you do, hold on to this one, and make sure that you don't take his support for granted. If you let him know that you're there for him the way he's there for you, then you guys will stay each other's biggest fans.

Mostly Cs: He has a walk-on role.

For whatever reason, this guy is acting more like a film crew member than your leading man. It's normal for you each to do your own thing from time to time, but your boyfriend is pretty much always taking himself out of whatever scene you're in. You can try telling him that you want him to be more involved in your life. But if that doesn't work, chances are he's too involved in himself right now to care about anyone else. If he's not willing to play a supporting role in your life, then he shouldn't get to play any role. And . . . cut!

37

Are you a MATERIAL girl?

Check out what your attitude toward money and status buys says about you.

1 What are your trips to the mall usually like?

A | All-out shopping bonanzas!

B | You try stuff on and hang out more than you actually shop.

C | You walk in, buy what you need, and walk out.

2 Your favorite shoes are:

A | The latest designer heels (you saw them on an actress and had to have them!).

| B | Cute sandals you bought at the mall. |
| C | The comfy, beat-up sneaks you've had forever. |

 3 **What happens to your paychecks?**

A	They fund your Louis Vuitton bag obsession.
B	You buy a few nice things but spend most of your money on going out with friends.
C	Every penny gets put away in your savings account.

 4 **What would you give up in exchange for five million dollars?**

A	Your best friend, chocolate, and the next year of your life. It'd be worth it!
B	That's a toughie. Maybe you'd give up dating until college . . . but maybe not!
C	Nothing . . . money doesn't mean anything to you.

5 **Do you think rich people are generally happier than poor people?**

A | Of course—they can buy whatever they want!

B | They have things easier, but money doesn't buy happiness.

C | No way—the more money you have, the more complicated your life is.

MOSTLY As: Money matters.

You place a ton of importance on the material things in life, like labels and luxury. It's not a bad thing to have high standards, but if you don't pay attention to the naturally good things you don't have to pay for, you're gonna miss out on a lot. So try to place more value on whether you truly like something, not how much it costs.

MOSTLY Bs: Balanced buyer.

You like nice stuff as much as the next girl, but you don't feel empty inside if you don't score the latest "it" bag or gadget, because you know there are more important things than money. You spend your cash sensibly and don't demand anything outrageous from people buying gifts for you. That balanced outlook on wealth will help you live life to the fullest, without dwelling on what you have and what you don't.

MOSTLY Cs: Just the basics.

You don't let material things control your life, which is cool, but you also tend to think of money as the enemy. It's *great* that you feel that what you have is already enough to make you happy, but don't let that stop you from striving for even more success in life. You don't have to work to be a mini–Donald Trump, just make sure you don't settle for less than you're capable of.

38

Do you freak guys out?

When you walk into the room, does your crush think, "She's sweet"—or "She's scary!"?

1 **You have a new crush on a guy in your youth group. During the meeting, you:**

A Secretly sign him up to serve on the same committee you're on, then send him an e-mail telling him not to be late to the next committee event.

B Try to sit near him and smile when you catch him looking at you.

C Be as quiet as possible to avoid making a fool of yourself at all costs.

2 You hear through the grapevine that this guy at school might have a crush on you. Your plan of action is to:

A Corner him the next time you see him and tell him to admit it, because you already know *everything* (whether you like him or not).

B Assume nothing. If you like him too, you'll be a little extraflirty with him. If not, you'll just act like you normally do.

C Avoid him when you see him coming. You're sure it's not true anyway.

3 When it comes to your love life, your friends have nicknamed you:

A Man-eater.

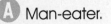 Flirt-master.

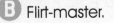 Wallflower.

4 You and your friends stop by the ice cream shop where your crush works. When it's time to order, you:

A Say, "Make me a sundae, sexy!", then tell him to come by your table to watch you tie the cherry stem into a knot with your tongue.

B Look him in the eye and say, "Hmmm . . . they all look good. What flavor would you get?"

C Chicken out and make your friend order your mint chocolate chip for you.

5 You and your new guy have only been dating for two months when his birthday rolls around. What do you have planned for his special day?

A Only a huge bash that he'll never forget. You've invited everyone at school and even enlisted his mom to invite all his relatives!

B You're baking him a batch of your special cookies, but that's it. The way you see it, it's too soon to buy him a big gift.

C Uh, maybe a card? He said he didn't want anything!

In your opinion, if you like a guy, nothing should hold you back from going for him. It's cool to be sure of yourself, but when you're way obvious about how much you're into him, it can backfire and actually turn your crush off. If you're into someone, try to let things play out naturally rather than plan ways to be close to him. That way he won't feel pressured, and you'll seem interested, not desperate and over-the-top!

You've got a good strategy going—you're a great flirt, but you don't overdo it. When you like a guy, you drop a few hints and then let him come to you. Guys love a challenge, so they flock right to your enchanting yet slightly mysterious vibe. You've got a nice way of putting a guy at ease, so your crush feels comfortable seeing where things go. To him, you seem like a fun girl he wants to get to know better, not a girl who's rushing him into anything.

Mostly Cs: Guys think, "Um, who is that girl?"

You're naturally shy when it comes to guys, and it's cool to want to be discreet. But if you never send your crush any signals that you're into him, he'll never even realize he's got a shot with you. You're always sneaking away or keeping quiet when he's around, so chances are he's totally oblivious to you. You don't need to vamp it up or anything, but try giving him little clues that you might be interested, like flashing a big smile or complimenting his shirt. Even a small gesture could start the flirtatious spark you need!

39

What do people say behind your back?

Everybody talks. And there are clues to what they're saying when *your* name comes up.

1] **You and your friends are clubbing, and everyone's curfew is almost up. You're the** one who:

A Gets dragged off the dance floor, still shaking your hips.

B Is rounding people up and making shopping plans for tomorrow.

C Went home about an hour ago.

2] You're having late-night fries with your friends at Denny's and in walks your crush with a group of his friends. You:

A Hop out of your seat, run over to him, and give him a big hug, telling him how hot he looks.

B Look over, flash a foxy smile, and wave.

C Stuff fries into your mouth and keep your eyes down.

3] It's the night before your English paper is due. Be honest . . . what are you most likely doing?

A Downing way too many Red Bulls and pulling one of your usual all-nighters, since you haven't even started.

B Reading over what you've already done and adding the finishing touches.

C Your other homework. You've been done with that paper for a week.

4] You heard that this girl at school is spreading a totally untrue rumor about you. What do you do about it?

A Get in her face and confront her after class. Then start a mean rumor about her on your blog.

B Wait till you can talk to her alone, then ask her what's up.

C Nothing. You figure it'll probably just fizzle out.

5] It's been a long week. What are you most looking forward to this weekend?

A Hitting as many parties as you can—it's how you unwind!

B Chilling with your friends or boyfriend (and probably putting off your homework till Sunday)!

C Plopping down on the couch in your jammies for a reality-TV marathon.

[Mostly As] "She's gonna burn out."

No one has ever accused you of being blasé. No matter what you do—date, argue, whatever—you do it with your trademark intensity. And while people are drawn to your passion and energy, they honestly get a little worried that you'll run out of steam, or worse, self-destruct. Plus, it can get a little tiring for them to always have to deal with your emergencies. Try to inject a little moderation in your life—not everything (like partying) has to be done to the extreme. Also, if you feel yourself getting worked up, take a deep breath and count to twenty before making a move. That trick helps take the urgency out of a situation and will help you stop yourself from stressing out over every little thing.

[Mostly Bs] "She's so together."

Your friends marvel at your ability to make it through any sticky situation while keeping your cool. Sure, you get stressed . . . who doesn't? But you always find a way to deal with your problems without boiling over. You know how to have fun, but you also know when to call it a night—and you never make your friends clean up your messes. If you see a friend who's having trouble dealing with stuff in her life with as much composure, offer her some advice. The world could use a little more of your unruffled mind-set!

[Mostly Cs] "She needs to live a little."

You're sweet and hardworking, but your friends may be concerned that you're not putting yourself "out there" enough. It's relaxing to chill by yourself, but you may find that you have way more fun if you hit a party now and then. And while you dig a sense of calm, try living on the edge just a little and do something unexpected (like flirting with your crush) now and then! Not only will people see you in a new light, but you might even start seeing yourself as more of the fun girl, not just the responsible one.

40

Should you **break up** with your friend?

She used to be your bff, but now you're not so sure. Find out if you should try to fix your friendship—or let it fall away.

1] **If you told her the cute guy you've been crushing on forever finally asked you to hang out, she'd probably say:**

A "I'm so happy for you . . . but isn't that guy kind of lame?"

B "I'm so happy for you . . . but I had no idea you liked him!"

C "I'm so happy for you . . . I knew he'd realize how awesome you are eventually!"

2 When just the two of you are hanging out, your conversation usually goes like this:

A She talks about her guy drama, her parent drama, etc., while you try to get a word in edgewise.

B You guys take turns catching up—it seems like so much has happened since you last hung out.

C You gab nonstop about last weekend's party, your crushes, your teachers . . . you guys could talk forever!

3 The last time you two got into a fight, it was because:

A You heard she was saying shady things about you to your other friends.

B She thought you were leaving her out of your life, or vice versa.

C She spaced when she said she'd e-mail you that picture of the two of you last weekend.

4] When you picture your relationship with her ten years from now, what do you see?

A To be honest, you're not sure if you'll still want her in your life. You already feel like you're over her sometimes.

B Your lives will take completely different paths, but you're sure you guys will still be in touch.

C You can't even imagine not talking to her every day like you do now.

5] The one thing about her that bugs you is:

A She makes fun of you in front of other people. She thinks she's being funny, but it's so not cool.

B She doesn't quite "get" you as much as some of your other friends do.

C There's not really one thing . . . she's got tons of minor quirks, but you love her anyway.

[Mostly As]

Yes—she doesn't have your back.

Even if her intentions seem good, this girl manages to make you feel pretty bad about yourself—and that's not what friendship is about. Maybe she feels threatened by your successes, or maybe she's just insecure about her own life, but it seems like she's always looking for little ways to undermine you. Whether she's sabotaging your love life or putting you down in public, her bad friend behavior isn't limited to one isolated incident—it seems to happen constantly. You don't need someone hanging around you who makes you question yourself. Tell her how you feel and cite specific incidents. Give her a week or two to prove that she can change. If she doesn't, it's time to retire this faux friendship and focus on your real ones.

> It seems like she's always looking for little ways to undermine you.

[Mostly Bs]
Maybe—your lives aren't in step.

It might be that you two used to be superclose, but it seems like lately, you've been growing apart. You've got different groups of friends, different schedules, and probably different styles— in fact, you don't remember when you two became such different people. But that doesn't mean you have to cut her out of your life completely. If you still care about her, you don't have to be besties, but make an effort to stay in touch and keep

Lately, you've been growing apart.

up with what's going on in her life. If you feel like trying to stay close is putting a strain on you, it might be best to go your separate ways. Phase her out slowly, while staying friendly and polite.

[Mostly Cs]
Nope—she's still your bff.

Your friendship is definitely the real deal. She's psyched for you when something great happens, and she's there for you when you're down. She's the first person you call when you want to make weekend plans, and lots of times, the last person you talk to before falling asleep. You guys are so close, it's like you can read each other's minds. It's great that you have someone who you know you can always count on, but try not to spend every waking moment with *just* her.

It's like you can read each other's minds.

Hang out with other people now and then—a little time apart will help prevent "friend burnout" and make you appreciate your amazing bond even more.

inner life

How well do you know yourself?

Have you thought about what *really* makes you tick? It's time to find out!

1) You're trying out a new restaurant with a group of girlfriends. The second you crack open the menu, your best friend says:

a) "If you could pick an entrée this *year*, that'd be great!"

b) "Hmmm . . . what looks good to you?"

c) "Lemme guess . . . you're getting the chicken, like you do everywhere else we go!"

2) When you try on clothes at the mall, how many items do you usually take into the dressing room with you?

a) As many as you can—you never know what will look good, so you try everything!

b) A few things that look like they're your style.

c) Um, you hardly ever try anything on. If you go shopping for a black top, you just grab a black top and go.

3) What did the last three guys you've had crushes on have in common?

a) Almost nothing. One was a jock, one was an artsy musician, and one was a brain. Go figure.

b) They all had a similar style and had a lot in common with you, like you loved all the same TV shows.

c) A *lot*. They looked and acted so much alike, they could have been triplets!

$4)$ **When family friends ask you what you want to be when you grow up, what do you tell them?**

a) "I have no idea. I'm not sure what I'd be best at yet."

b) "I have some ideas . . . maybe a vet or a social worker. I love the idea of making the world a better place."

c) "A photojournalist. No question in my mind."

$5)$ **When you take quizzes like this, do you have an idea of which category you'll end up in even before you get to the end?**

a) Nope. Most of the time, my category surprises me!

b) Usually. But I still like to take them . . . sometimes I learn something new about myself.

c) Every single time. Sometimes I just skip the questions altogether and just read the category that matches me best.

Mostly As Self searching.

You're still trying to figure out who you are, which is totally cool. You're young, so no one expects you to know what career you want or even to have a go-to guy type. But getting to know yourself better makes life a little easier, because you can narrow down your options when facing a tough decision. To become more familiar with the inner you, make lists of stuff you know you love and don't love—like your favorite qualities in friends and guys, your least-favorite foods, the colors that look best on you, etc. Looking at them will help you put your tastes in perspective. So next time you're faced with a daunting selection at the mall, you'll be able to skip past the generic stuff to something that's more you!

Mostly Bs Self smart.

You have a great sense of who you are and what you stand for, but you're not afraid to branch out from your usual type of guy or menu favorite and see what else is out there. When it comes to your future, you already have some idea of where you're going, which gives you a great head start in life. Your friends love that you're so secure in yourself and what you value—and your ability to still shake it up every now and then.

Mostly Cs Self stubborn.

You like what you like, you hate what you hate, and no one's changing your mind about any of it. It's great that you're sure of yourself, but it's possible that you're too set in your ways. You have a long life ahead of you, and if you're already done exploring your tastes, the years ahead might be pretty boring (and people might start seeing you as dull!). Even if you think you won't like it, veer away from your set-in-stone tastes and try something new once in a while. Salmon instead of chicken? Skinny instead of boot-cut? Who knows—you just might discover a new favorite, or ten!

Marina Khidekel's obsession with quizzes started in middle school, as a direct result of her not being allowed to read the teen magazines they were published in. So of course she ended up working for them—and writing quizzes. After interning at *Jane*, Marina went on to work at *YM*, MTV Networks, and *CosmoGIRL!*, writing and editing news, relationship, and feature stories—and fueling the introspective fires of teens everywhere.